This

Special

Gift

From

_____

To

_____

Date

_____

LOCATING
YOUR SCRIPT
IN THE
SCRIPTURE

'WALE ORELESI

February 2015 Locating your script in the scripture

© 'Wale Orelesi

Published by Divine Grace Enterprises Limited, London.

DIVINE GRACE
ENTERPRISES LIMITED.
"For with Grace Enterprises, nothing shall be impossible"

www.divinegraceenterprise.com

ISBN: 978-1-909206-12-0

Cover Design by:

Zoe Communications Limited.

Unless where otherwise stated; all bible passages are taken from the NIV version of the Holy Bible.

ENDORSEMENTS FOR LOCATING YOUR SCRIPTS IN THE SCRIPTURE

The Unique presentation of the revelations in this book is one of the main attractions for me.

Many see drama as 'play'. But drama is more than play, it is the mind of God to His people.

Pastor Wale uses drama to draw an analogy of how we are to fulfil destiny and purpose. This book is a must read. I recommend it to all.

Rev. David Kolawole Okeowo
TRECOM INT'L., London.

Locating your script from the scripture is a cry of the spirit to see men and women of God rise up, occupy their God ordained position in destiny and finish strong.

This master piece presents Pastor Adewale Orelesi as an astute teacher of the word who researches the scripture to bring out hidden treasures for day to day living. The book contains priceless and uncommon insights, and can prove to be the next springboard that you require in order to discover, pursue and fulfill God's script for your life.

Let the simple read and get wise, let the strong read and take heed, and let the aged read and finish strong!

The depth of insight and revelation of God's purpose that are contained in the pages of this book will be a great source of blessing and inspiration to the body of Christ.

Fisayo Daramola *Ph.D*
Covenant University
Canaan Land, Ogun State.

Locating your script in the scriptures is a master piece. Pastor Wale Orelesi in this awesome work clearly unveils God's purpose for our lives and how we can find, and chart our course in the road to divine destiny.

As you travel through this life changing book you must get ready not only to be illuminated by the divine truths and insights therein but also to be transformed into a whole new you, armed with wisdom, purpose and understanding yourself and the world that is already awaiting your manifestation.

Pastor Benjamin Kwentua
CEO, Purpose Track Consulting/Purpose Track Christian Centre, Johannesburg, South Africa.

Pastor Wale Orelesi, in this book, LOCATING YOUR SCRIPT IN THE SCRIPTURE unveiled to us that our destiny in God can only be pursued and be fulfilled only after we have discovered it. He did not just write the book from head knowledge but out of personal experience, as he is a good example of a purpose driven life.

Thank you my dear brother and friend, for this insightful dramatic narration of a life of purpose through this wonderful masterpiece.

A must read for everyone ready to live out their God ordained destiny.

Samuel Oyeleke
*Pastor in Charge,
RCCG, Citadel of His Glory,
Festac Town, Lagos - Nigeria.*

'Wale Orelesi has done a great job in this book "Locating your script in the Scripture". He has brought an entirely different and unique approach to the teaching of purpose. Its a must-read for anyone who desires to influence his or her world positively.

Kunle Joe Komolafe
Conference Speaker, Life Coach and Leadership Consultant! CEO, Crecon.

Like Shakespeare said, "All of life is a stage", this book uses the metaphor of a theater to illustrate the journey of purpose. Herein is truth that can set you free – free to fulfill your destiny – by helping you locate your script.

The volume you have in your hands is simply written, and I dare say, in almost two decades of teaching the same subject, this comes with a refreshing perspective. In unmistakable terms, the unique insights clearly elucidate the subject of divine purpose from the Scriptures.

A good book should not necessarily expound new ideas or things I have never heard before. Some of the best books I have read (and I have read quite some volumes in my life and career as a pastor, public speaker and leadership consultant) sheds new light on truth already revealed to us. "Then said a teacher, 'Speak to us of teaching; and he said: "No man can reveal to you anything but that which already lies half asleep in the dawning of your knowledge!" This book spoke to me and I am sure it will speak to you of the things you already 'know'. That in my opinion is the best part of the deal in taking your time to read and study this book.

I am happy to recommend this book. Read and study it for your learning and apply it to your life and ministry. If you are ready, locate your script, and get set. "Camera! Light! Action!"

Rev. Yomi Olufiade
Conference Speaker, Bible Teacher
& Leadership Consultant Abuja, Nigeria.

CONTENTS

DEDICATION

This book is dedicated to God - Almighty Father, Jesus Christ - the Living Word of God, The gentle Holy Spirit - the comforter, and all the saints in light.

For this inspiration all glory, honor, and adoration, I return to you, my father, and my God.

And also to **Rev. Tony Akinyemi** and **Rev. Funke Felix - Adejumo** for inspiring this work through their many books I have been priviledged to publish.

ACKNOWLEDGEMENTS

Every good and perfect gift indeed comes from above. I will forever be grateful to God for helping me to locate my script in the Holy Scriptures. I acknowledge His bountiful grace and call upon my life; Lord to you alone I return all the glory. I couldn't have done this without having you as my source.

I know I obtained favor from God when I found Ibiyinka Arinola. You are my friend and a lover of my destiny, thank you for being my number one fan and a loving and caring mother of our four great children. Being my wife has made my life meaningful and fruitful in so many ways that words cannot describe! You are the costliest of all rare pearls!

My team: Zoe, Hadassah, Sharon and Debrah; thank you for being teachable and God loving. Your understanding of ministry early is a plus to my calling and parental style. You are such great gifts coming from my loins!

To all who have at one point or the other played a lead role in my life's journey: Rev. Tony Akinyemi and his amiable wife Pst Tutu; thanks for giving me the platform to declare the whole counsel of God to God's people in Akowonjo. I count it as a great privilege to be a vessel in the hands of the Master to bless lives here. I deeply and sincerely appreciate the entire ministers, workers and all members of TSF Akowonjo; thanks for accepting me and my message; it has been a big boost to my ministry.

Rev. Kola Okeowo, Evang. Mike Bamiloye, Dr. Fisayo Daramola, Pst. Benjamin Kwentua, Elder Ernest Mbanefo: a million thanks for helping to nurture and fan the flame of grace upon my life.

My big uncles: Alaga Remi Ajala, Pst. Bimbo Oludara, Pst. Jimi and Laide Adeyemo, Elder David Adegbite, Pst. Olu Awogbemila, Pst. Lekan Adeleke, Mr. Lanre Fasakin, Pastor Sean Akinrele: thanks for being such a good example to believers. Your lives are molding great men!

My fellow TSF parish pastors: Nehemiah Akanbi, Lekan Omisope, Toyin Adebowale, Joe Olutuase, Kingsley Simon, Simbo Oni, Kayode Braimoh, Toyin Kehinde, Dr. Odumade, Cornelius Adewale. I appreciate you all for contributing to this work in no small measure; you will not lose your reward in Jesus name.

My covenant friends: Pastor Sam Oyeleke, Pastor Praise Ayodele, Rev. Debo Adedeji, Pastor Wale Adeshina, Pastor Matthew Babalola, Pastor Olu Adebayo, Pastor Deji Alabi, Pastor 'Wole Abayomi, Engr. Bisi Ologunleko, Bro. Remi Adesola May the Lord bless you real good!

FOREWORD 1

The Holy Bible is also refered to as the Holy Scriptures because it is indeed a Holy Script that has been written by God to give directions and purpose to our lives.

Jesus Christ our Lord said, "it is written in the volumes of the Book concerning me..." In the same vein, God has documented so much concerning each one of us in the Holy scriptures. Jesus refused to fulfill in His life whatever was not in the Holy script. He did all things – from His virgin birth to His crucifixion, resurrection, and ascension to heaven – only according to the SCRIPTURES.

Wale Orelesi, in this apt treatise, has laid out for us in very clear and compelling language, how each one of us too may locate our roles in the SCRIPT that God has written concerning us and fulfill it while time lasts. May this work inspire, challenges, and motivate every reader to find their roles in the SCRIPT and receive grace, strength, and courage to fulfill it.

I highly recommend this work to every man and woman of destiny. Live and make a mark.

Tony Akinyemi
Senior Pastor,
The Shepherd's Flock International Church

FOREWORD 2

A scene unfolded in Bethlehem Judea, a young lad was panting as he ran to rescue a helpless sheep from its predator; a merciless lion.

(1 Samuel 17:34-37)
David courageously performed the feat knowing fully well that the God of his fathers had ordained and empowered him to 'live the Script' written about him. He intuitively understood that no matter what... It must end well.

> **And we know that all things work together for good to them that love God, to them who are the called according to his purpose.** Romans 8:28

His time in the bush was to prepare him for the ultimate assignment; being the Shepherd of Israel.

David's purpose brought him before kings, gave him an inheritance among the great, made him the greatest king in Israel and gave him eternal relevance.

The script of my life opened on a platform of mercy, against all odds, God anointed me to distribute inheritances to His people- help women achieve the plans of God for their lives; help them preserve the destinies and future of their seed and help men enjoy the best in their family life. This I understand and it continually keeps me on my toes.

As I play out my script, as directed by the Holy Ghost (who is the Master and Lead Director) I realized that a person can live to be a hundred years , eat, drink and sleep, live in the nicest house and drive the best cars and still not play out the script written by God for his destiny.

'Wale Orelesi in this well-researched and articulated book has proved that getting involved in various activities does not mean that a person is fulfilling divine agenda. **Busyness is not tantamount to fruitfulness.**

Fulfilling God's purpose requires the understanding of your life's assignment and running with the consciousness of destiny. This will give you peace, divine resources, make you a king and enthrone you on the palace designed for you. There are men who are ordained to sit in political palaces but are mediocres in businesses and vice-versa.

As you read this powerful book I pray that you will discover your divine script, interpret your part correctly and play it excellently. May the God of all grace strengthen you. And may you not run behind schedule!

Funke Felix - Adejumo

Funke Felix-Adejumo Foundation,
Nigeria. 2015

INTRODUCTION

Nothing about our lives can ever take God by surprise. He knows all things and He sees the end from the very beginning.

A man went to a cinema to watch a thrilling movie so full of suspense that it kept everybody at the edge of their seats. While people were agitated and worried over what would happen to the movie's protagonist, whose life was in danger, there in midst of the nervous audience, was another man seated calmly and eating popcorn.

While the intrigue was on, the man eating popcorn was as calm as ever. A man seated beside him couldn't take it anymore and in anger asked, Don't you have human feelings at all'? How could you be so unmoved?' The man smiled, looked at him and said 'I wrote the script. He will survive the crisis.' The previously angered man now smiled, became more relaxed and also ordered for popcorn.

Esther was an orphan and by virtue of the fact that she had no parental covering, it was enough to judge and conclude that she could never go far in life. Humanly speaking, she stood no chance to live an impactful life. But God has chosen the foolish things of the world to confound the wise. He has also made the weak things of the world to put to shame the things loaded with might and great strength.

When her parents died, Mordecai her uncle took up the responsibility of raising her. They were taken as captives and carried away from Jerusalem. In Babylon they were 'illegal immigrants.' They were treated as second class citizens and were in no way entitled to the good life enjoyed by the citizens. In spite of these, they were still happy to live in that land and get by.

Until an enemy rose up...

This enemy decided to completely wipe out the entire Jewish race in the land. This evil was orchestrated by Haman who was the king's right hand man. Before he could execute this plan he had to get the king's permission and he went all the way to ensure it was turned into law; a strong one that cannot be altered, sealed by the king's ring.

So the king took his signet ring from his finger

and gave it to Haman son of Hammedatha, the Agagite, the enemy of the Jews. "Keep the money," the king said to Haman, "and do with the people as you please."-Esther 3:10-11(NIV)

In the days in which the Jews lived in that land, anything signed and sealed by the king's ring was unchangeable. Once the writing is signed, it becomes a decree that cannot be changed, according to the law of the Medes and Persians. It was a verdict that could not be altered; for no reason whatsoever.

By the time the decree went out that all the Jews must be wiped out, Esther was already a queen in the king's palace. She was in a safe and comfortable zone; far from the plague of the sword. She could decide not to interfere with her race's welfare since she could be immune to the king's order. However, Mordecai said something to her...

"...Do not think that because you are in the king's house you alone of all the Jews will escape. For if you remain silent at this time, relief and deliverance for the Jews will arise from another place, but you and your father's family will perish. And who knows but that you have come to your royal position for such a time as this?"-Esther 4:13-14(NIV).

Mordecai's question to Esther was a pointer to her life's purpose. That was the role God designed for her to play. She was sent to deliver her people because God knew that a time like this would come for the Jews to need a 'saviour.' She came on the scene to preserve the Jewish race! Everything she experienced earlier in life prior to her ascension as Queen of Persia were just auditions; getting her ready to key into her destiny.

It was while she was living with her uncle that she was introduced to the God of Israel. She was raised to understand that there is a God in heaven who rules in the affairs of men. Not only that, she knew that the arm of flesh would fail, that explained why it never crossed her mind to use her beauty and royal position to bargain for the lives of her people. She sought the Ultimate Power that rules the entire world and the kingdoms in it. She was ready to pay for the ransom of her people with her life, hence her audacious phrase- 'if I perish I perish!' What a resolution!

When she presented her case to the Ruler of all nations, she obtained God's favour that made her husband, the king hold out the royal sceptre to her. Her race was preserved and the intention of God for creating her was fulfilled.

Your life has a purpose attached to it. You may not understand all that is taking place now, things may not follow your carefully laid out plans; the enemy could have unleashed terror on you, but you know what? God will make everything work out for your good and fit into His eternal counsel.

Joseph also didn't stand a chance at all in playing a role on the national scene in Egypt. He was an ex-convict, yet God used him to change the course of history and preserved a nation during famine.

Rahab was a prostitute but she crossed over to the army of God and became a part of God's grand scheme of things-she became an ancestress of Jesus Christ.

> *Salmon the father of Boaz, whose mother was Rahab, Boaz the father of Obed, whose mother was Ruth, Obed the father of Jesse, and Jesse the father of King David.*-Matthew 1:5-6(NIV)

Paul was a terrorist, yet he wrote more than half of all the books in the New Testament.

The question of purpose, God's eternal plan and original counsel, is as old as time itself. No man that ever walked on earth was born for no reason. We all came to do something.

God has designed the part He wants us to play in His eternal plan for mankind.
Our lives began in God; and He planned the details of all

our days even before we were born. Before we live a single day out of all the years assigned to our existence, He sees and knows what will happen in each of them.

> *'Your eyes saw my unformed body; all the days ordained for me were written in your book before one of them came to be'*-Psalm 139:16 (NIV)

Events predate us. There was something in the heart of God before He took time to create each and every one of us for a unique purpose.

He made us for a specific purpose and we must embrace His plans for our lives. The day you discover why you are here and begin to walk in it, is the day you start living. If you are yet to do this, then you merely exist on the face of the earth.

> *'Then said I, Lo, I come (in the volume of the book it is written of me,) to do thy will, O God. Then said he, Lo, I come to do thy will, O God...'*
> Heb.10:7,9. (KJV)

God has given us a body, time and a geographical zone to play our part in His eternal scheme of things.

The Master of all ages has a lead role designed for you. He has placed the script in your own hands and the set designed to bring you on scene. Are you ready to step up to the challenge? There are things to do and places to go; God's Spirit beckons!

YOU
PASSED
THE AUDITION

"Dreams are like the paints of a great artist. Your dreams are your paints, the world is your canvas. Believing, is the brush that converts your dreams into a masterpiece of reality."
- thinkexist.com

YOU PASSED
THE AUDITION

There are certain bible passages that I enjoy reading. Apart from the message they convey, their sentence construction is simple and easy to grasp; leading me to discover eternal truths. I must confess that the first chapter of the gospel of Matthew is not one of them; until I get to verse sixteen, I don't seem to understand why all these names were penned down. A similar set of names were also set out in Luke 3:23-38. All you get to read is 'begat after begat'.

Until recently, they were just a dull string of names I always skipped reading.

I now understand that each of us is a master-piece.

However, as unexciting as this list of names may be, each soul, each individual mentioned there was part of an orchestra. They each combined in their own unique ways and played their role to fit into a larger production.

The Holy Spirit of God opened my eyes to see that none of the men whose name was mentioned in that scripture is irrelevant in His purpose. They all fit into a specific role; which none other except them could fill. Another thing I learnt is that failure to fulfil your role may hinder or slow other people down from fulfilling theirs.

YOU ARE A MASTER-PIECE

You are a being like no other. You stand out in no small way from all the millions of people walking on planet earth. Your finger print, your eyes, your voice, and a

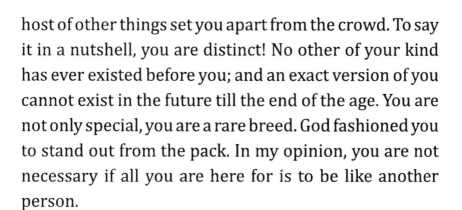

You stand out in no small way from all the millions of people walking on planet earth.

host of other things set you apart from the crowd. To say it in a nutshell, you are distinct! No other of your kind has ever existed before you; and an exact version of you cannot exist in the future till the end of the age. You are not only special, you are a rare breed. God fashioned you to stand out from the pack. In my opinion, you are not necessary if all you are here for is to be like another person.

YOU ARE A PERSON OF PURPOSE

Conception goes beyond a man lying with a woman to

produce a baby. It is a miracle. It is astonishing to discover that this miracle involves the cast of a million of spermatozoa fighting to fertilize an egg. Yet in this fight only one will come out victorious. That proves to me that being conceived in your mother's womb came by divine selection. You beat the odds and came into being because God knew that you perfectly fit into His grand scheme of operations. Even from conception, you are invaluable! If God didn't want you; you wouldn't have been. You are required to effect changes here and get something done.

God chose you based on His judgment that you are qualified. The thought of being selected and chosen by God is enough reason to let you know that you are here on a mission.

The counsel and purpose of God cannot exist and be fulfilled in a vacuum. He needs vessels that can bear His glory. He wants hands that can heal, mouths that can testify of His love and make manifest His compassion. God needs a medium through which His eternal power can travel. Like electricity, the current must flow through a conduit to get power generated and become usable.

Man was created by God for a reason. As a matter of truth, everything on earth and in heaven is made for a purpose. You need to clearly understand that God is the God of purpose who does nothing without an aim. In that vein, you are also a creation of purpose. He didn't just create you to occupy space and live in time. He made you to fit into a role; specifically scripted for you.

His purpose for your life must be played out; in the very same way He wants it. You passed the audition and came at the right time. You came on set; just at the right time that God would have you to be alive in history. God gave you the perfect body for your role. He has a place where you fit into perfectly. These things were determined by His design, concept and a purpose that must not be thwarted. You are constantly on His mind. He is looking for how His plans for you can come into being. He has pretty good plans for you.

> *"For I know the plans I have for you," declares the Lord, "plans to prosper you and not to harm you, plans to give you hope and a future"*- Jer. 29:11(NIV)

All the thoughts of God towards you are thoughts of

He didn't just create you to occupy space and live in time. He made you to fit into a role; specifically scripted for you.

peace. Sometimes you go through unpleasant

31

situations that make you begin to wonder, 'Does God really care?' You could have challenges that are as hot as the furnace and it seems God is quiet. His seeming silence is not because He doesn't care about what you are going through; it is just that He knows that whatever comes your way will work for your overall good.

> *'And we know that all things work together for good to them that love God, to them who are the called according to his purpose.'*
> Rom.8:28. (KJV)

DIVINE SELECTION-THE CAST AND CREW

> *Not only that, but Rebekah's children were conceived at the same time by our father Isaac. Yet, before the twins were born or had done anything good or bad-in order that God's purpose in election might stand: not by works but by Him who calls she was told, "The older will serve the younger." Just as it is written: "Jacob I loved, but Esau I hated."*
> -Rom.9:10-13-(NIV)

> *'And Samuel said unto Jesse, are here all thy children? And he said, there remaineth yet the youngest, and, behold, he keepeth the sheep. And Samuel said unto Jesse, send and fetch him: for we will not sit down till he come hither. And*

he sent, and brought him in. Now he was ruddy, and withal of a beautiful countenance, and goodly to look to. And the Lord said, arise, anoint him: for this is he.' 1 Sam.16:11-12. (KJV)

When Rebecca gave birth to Jacob and Esau, there was a combat regarding who wanted to come out first. One outsmarted the other and became the elder. Amazingly enough, God indicated His preference for the younger one much earlier. Does that mean He is partial? Well, that answers to the question of divine selection. It is only the sovereign God that can explain the details behind His choice.

The Scripture above goes to prove that God makes choices. He selects the people who works for Him and that is a pointer that before you were selected there are others that could have gone for that specific 'role'. Instead God chose you. When He chose you He knew that when the appointed time comes for you to do what you've been called to do, all things will fall in place and

> He knows that whatever comes your way will work for your overall good.

you will take charge at that point in order to manifest what God has placed in you to bless your generation with.

Nothing takes God by surprise. No event shocks Him. The Bible says He sees the end from the beginning. He knows what will happen before it eventually does. That explains why the Bible says Jesus Christ; the son of God is the lamb slain before the foundation of the earth. See Revelations 13:8.

God knew that Adam and Eve would fall short so He made provision in Jesus Christ for the atonement of their sin. He put in place the plan of redemption ever before it came to pass.

God saw the famine in Egypt before Joseph was born. He saw Goliath defying the army of Israel before time began.

He knew that Judas Iscariot would betray Jesus. He knew what would happen per time in each scene and He has stationed His trained actors who will perfectly interpret the roles and bring Him glory.

OVERVIEW

Your life is not a mistake. God chose you before the beginning of time to fulfil a unique assignment and you will do well to discover it. Your body frame, the time you were born and the family you were born into were carefully chosen by Him to fit into what you came to do on earth. Nothing about your life is an accident.

REFLECTION

I) Do you like yourself, the family you were born into and the circumstances surrounding your birth? If the answer is no to any of these, you need to know that you have little or no influence over them and in spite of how ugly they may be, you can still break barriers and fulfill purpose in spite of all odds.

ii) Do you tend to blame others or yourself for the setbacks that you have encountered in life? If yes, then you must know that in order to fulfill purpose you need to shed off unnecessary excess luggage and travel light. If you don't, your journey will be slow and very painful. Forgive yourself and others and press on for the beautiful future ahead of you.

BEFORE GOD SETS THE STAGE

"Before I shaped you in the womb, I knew all about you. Before you saw the light of day, I had holy plans for you: A prophet to the nations - that's what I had in mind for you." Jer. 1:5 (The Message)

BEFORE GOD
SETS THE STAGE

There is no corporate organization that exists without having a standard and concise vision and mission statement. The vision is the aim, goal and objective of that organization and the mission statement is how the organization sets to achieve it; plus the compelling line that will drive it. This is to help the organization identify what it stands for and how to aim to achieve the essence of being in operation. More often than not, the vision and mission statement are stated in clear terms and made known to everybody connected to the organization in one way or the other.

In the same vein, there is something about you that sets you apart from other similar entities; it is your script. It is what you are here to be and do. It also contains the step by step processes that will be required to achieve that aim. Before God introduces you on stage, He will first of all offer you the script wherein lies your purpose on earth.

Lights, Camera, Action!

After coming in contact with your script, God will ensure you pass through a preparatory stage. This is the stage where you are refined for your role before you are placed on set and the camera starts rolling. Moses had to be separated from the luxury of Pharaoh's palace to lead his father-in-law's flock in preparation for the ultimate goal of leading God's people to the Promised Land.

David was entrusted with his father's flock before he could mount the throne. He was so passionate about his shepherd duties that he rescued his sheep from a lion and a bear. That was the heart God wanted to develop in him; a heart that will stop at nothing to see to the welfare and good governance of His people.

There is something about you that sets you apart from other similar entities; it is your script.
It is what you are here to be and do

Joseph was trained in administrative skills and issues of integrity at Potiphar's house and in the prison before he became Egypt's prime minister. Sometimes what we are going through may look odd and of great pain but they are being used by God to have us trained for the role He has scripted for our lives.

39

LOCATING THE SCRIPT - ITS ESSENCE

Life is like a movie and things don't just fall in place. A lot goes into a good movie production. The concept must be clearly stated, the stage set and each player carefully selected, auditioned and chosen for the role they are playing. The lighting must be perfect, the director must be on point and the message clearly passed to the intended audience. Above all, interpreting the role must leave a mark that will not be forgotten in a hurry.

No matter how skilful an actor is, he must first come in contact with the script. A thorough study of the script makes things become clearer to the actor. Sad though, it is not every man that discovers purpose. Some do yet they are unable to fulfil it. It is only a few that are able to discover and fulfil their purpose.

Your life has value. It has a purpose; you must live it out. But you will remain in the dark until you lay your hands on the script that clearly states your role in destiny.

There are three plans that have been mapped out for you in life.

1. **God's plan** for you (to fulfil purpose)
2. **Satan's plan** for you (to fail in discovering /fulfilling your purpose)
3. **Your plan** for you (allowing God's plan or that of

the devil come to pass).

It is the situation of one life, three plans.

'For unto us a child is born, unto us a son is given: and the government shall be upon his shoulder: and his name shall be called Wonderful, Counsellor, the mighty God, the everlasting Father, the Prince of Peace. Of the increase of his government and peace there shall be no end...' Isaiah 9:6. (KJV)

'The spirit of the Lord God is upon me; because the Lord hath anointed me to preach good tidings unto the meek; he hath sent me to bind up the brokenhearted, to proclaim liberty to the captives, and the opening of the prison to them that are bound; to proclaim the acceptable year of the Lord, and the day of vengeance of our God; to comfort all that mourn; to appoint unto them that mourn in Zion, to give unto them beauty for ashes, the oil of joy for mourning, the garment of praise for the spirit of heaviness; that they might be called trees of righteousness, the planting of the Lord, that he might be glorified.'
Isaiah 61:1-3. (KJV)

41

'And he came to Nazareth, where he had been brought up and, as his custom was, he went into the synagogue on the sabbath day, and stood up for to read. And there was delivered unto him the book of the prophet Esaias. And when he had opened the book, he found the place where it was written, the Spirit of the Lord is upon me, because he hath anointed me to preach the gospel to the poor; he hath sent me to heal the brokenhearted, to preach deliverance to the captives, and recovering of sight to the blind, to set at liberty them that are bruised, to preach the acceptable year of the Lord. And he closed the book, and he gave it again to the minister, and sat down. And the eyes of all them that were in the synagogue were fastened on him.' Luke 4:16-20. (KJV)

Your life has value. It has a purpose; you must live it out. But you will remain in the dark until you lay your hands on the script that clearly states your role in destiny.

Before Jesus was born, there were so many prophecies that came ahead of Him. There was a prophecy that stated the specific tribe He was going to come from. Ahead of His birth, His name was given to His parents and His ultimate essence for being birthed was tagged to the name.

42

"But you, Bethlehem Ephrathah, though you are small among the clans of Judah, out of you will come for me one who will be ruler over Israel, whose origins are from of old, from ancient times."-Micah 5:2(NIV)

'For to us a child is born, to us a son is given, and the government will be on his shoulders. And he will be called Wonderful Counselor, Mighty God, Everlasting Father, Prince of Peace....'-Isaiah 9:6(NIV)

'...an angel of the Lord appeared to him in a dream and said, "Joseph son of David, do not be afraid to take Mary home as your wife, because what is conceived in her is from the Holy Spirit. She will give birth to a son, and you are to give him the name Jesus, because he will save his people from their sins." All this took place to fulfil what the Lord had said through the prophet: "The virgin will conceive and give birth to a son, and they will call him Immanuel" (which means "God with us").- Mathew 1:20-23(NIV)

Nothing about His life came unannounced. His life had a direct flow of purpose, script and the other mechanisms earlier discussed. If the Messiah couldn't fulfil His purpose without a script; what makes you think you can stay afloat without one? There is no way you can play your role without a script.

Coming in contact with your script is like an estranged traveller coming in contact with a map. It will have two effects on him; first he could decide to just ignore it and continue to walk on. Secondly, he could see it as a pointer to where he is heading for. He has a choice - to either follow it or ignore it.

The onus rests on you to discover the script written concerning you. It is your sole responsibility and duty to painstakingly discover what the script says and read it thoroughly. You can do nothing without locating your script! You must search it out and sit down to read what has been written concerning you. The word of God says: *if the trumpet does not produce a distinct sound how will people prepare for war?* (I Cor.14:8) Direction is key and it comes when there is a definite route to follow to achieve a desired result.

Coming in contact with your script is like an estranged traveller coming in contact with a map.

Before you know the direction to head in life the trumpet must produce a DISTINCT sound. There must be clarity of purpose. Jesus couldn't start out in His calling until He saw the place where it was written concerning Him. After discovering His written out purpose, He connected immediately; and that is how it works for everybody. He brought what was written in the book of Isaiah to life in the temple when He read out His vision to the people present there that day.

Your life counts and that is simply because you are playing a lead role. You will do yourself a world of favour to discover this. This can only be done by being intimate with the script written concerning your role. Jesus said *'the Spirit of the Lord is upon me and He has anointed me to....'* When He discovered where it was written, He brought out what was written concerning Him. What has God anointed you to achieve for Him? What is your mandate on earth? Why are you here? What problems are you here to solve? What impact are you here to make?

The question of purpose...

You carry God's anointing for a cause, discover it. You were born for a purpose; search it out.

Let's go further and look at other people apart from the Saviour who also searched out the scripts written concerning them.

Before John the Baptist was born, there was a prophecy concerning his life. He knew exactly what he was born

Your life counts and that is simply because you are playing a lead role

to do and that helped him a great deal.

'But the angel said to him: "Do not be afraid, Zechariah; your prayer has been heard. Your wife Elizabeth will bear you a son, and you are to call him John. He will be a joy and delight to you, and many will rejoice because of his birth, for he will be great in the sight of the Lord. He is never to take wine or other fermented drink, and he will be filled with the Holy Spirit even before he is born. He will bring back many of the people of Israel to the Lord their God. And he will go on before the Lord, in the spirit and power of Elijah, to turn the hearts of the parents to their children and the disobedient to the wisdom of the righteous—to make ready a people prepared for the Lord."-Luke 1:13-17(NIV)

'There was a man sent from God whose name was John. He came as a witness to testify concerning that Light, so that through him all

46

might believe. He himself was not the light; he came only as a witness to the Light.'
-John 1:6-8(NIV)

'Finally they said, "Who are you? Give us an answer to take back to those who sent us. What do you say about yourself?" John replied in the words of Isaiah the prophet, "I am the voice of one calling in the wilderness, 'Make straight the way for the Lord.'"- John 1:22-23(NIV)

At a time, John was mistaken for the Messiah and he was almost accorded the honour due that office. But because he knew ahead of time that he was preparing the ground for the Messiah, he was able to keep his focus on his life's purpose. Your script will not only help you to discover purpose, it will greatly enhance your focus on it.

The word of God is light; it will illuminate your path. When you take time to study the scriptures you will discover amazing things. It will yield great results. Your success hinges on how you treat the word of God.

'Keep this Book of the Law always on your lips; meditate on it day and night, so that you may be careful to do everything written in it. Then

you will be prosperous and successful.' -Joshua 1:8(NIV)

'Your word is a lamp for my feet, a light on my path.' Psalms 119:105(NIV)

Your future is guaranteed by how much you love and

Your script will not only help you to discover purpose, it will greatly enhance your focus on it.

study the word of God. If you pay close attention to it, you can be sure that you are going to have good success. If you don't give it first place in your life; you will truncate the plan and purpose of God for you.

Another man that was able to chart another cause for his life based on God's word was Daniel. He discovered the plan that God had for his nation through the script written ahead of time. It was after understanding what was to take place that he began to pray and intercede that the eternal counsel of God for that situation will prevail.

> *In the first year of his reign, I, Daniel, understood from the Scriptures, according to the word of the Lord given to Jeremiah the prophet, that the desolation of Jerusalem would last seventy years. So I turned to the Lord God and pleaded with him in prayer and*

petition, in fasting, and in sackcloth and ashes.
I prayed to the Lord my God and confessed...'
Daniel 9:2-4(NIV)

The fulfilment of purpose begins when you discover what has been written concerning you. It doesn't stop there; discovering it should propel you to work towards fulfilling it. One of the ways you can effectively do that is to write out what the script says about you. In doing so, your mind will immediately start planning on how to get things rolling.

Then the Lord replied: "Write down the revelation and make it plain on tablets so that a herald may run with it. For the revelation awaits an appointed time; it speaks of the end and will not prove false. Though it lingers, wait for it; it will certainly come and will not delay. Habakkuk 2:2-3(NIV)

Keeping record will greatly help you to measure your progress. What gets measured gets done. If you don't have an aim you will meet no target. Your energy and resources will not be properly channelled and it will be easy to get distracted if you don't have a record of what God said before you came.

Nothing about your life will function by default. You must work it out. A lazy man stands no chance of fulfilling purpose. You must be ready to work.

> *That person is like a tree planted by streams of water, which yields its fruit in season and whose leaf does not wither—whatever they do prospers.-* Psalm 1:3(NIV)

To prosper means to succeed; to blossom and thrive. It means to have a positive result in an event undertaken. You must do something before the prosperity of God can rest on the work of your hands. When you do something in line with your purpose according to God's

 Keeping record will greatly help you to measure your progress.

design, He will make it prosper.

Measuring your growth on the purpose chart will make it easy for you to know the miles you have covered and what needs to get done. You must take responsibility for your destiny.

POINTERS TO DESTINY

'Call to me and I will answer you and tell you great and unsearchable things you do not know.'- Jeremiah 33:3(NIV)

It is not the plan of God to keep you in the dark. He promised to lead you in the best pathway for your life. Information enlightens your mind and keeps you in the know as to what should be done per time. Illumination occurs when light comes on a part of your life that gets you confused and wondering where to turn, who to call and what to do.

"Your word is a lamp for my feet and a light for my path"-Psalms 119:105(NIV)

Direction is crucial because it is when you know where to turn that your journey in life gets easy. Imagine driving a car with faulty windscreen wipers in a heavy downpour. How smooth would that journey be? Imagine having to drive through a dark thick forest at night without the car headlights on!

How would a pilot feel if he suddenly discovers he can't pick signals from the control tower? That is definitely a danger signal. In life, it is a jungle out there and we will do well to ask God to light our path and lead us in the right direction.

> **'Pray that the Lord your God will tell us where we should go and what we should do.'** - Jeremiah 42:3(NIV)

> **'Whether you turn to the right or to the left, your ears will hear a voice behind you, saying, "This is the way; walk in it.'** -Isaiah 30:21(NIV)

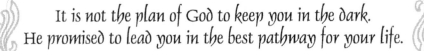

It is not the plan of God to keep you in the dark. He promised to lead you in the best pathway for your life.

> **'Trust in the Lord with all your heart and lean not on your own understanding; in all your ways submit to him, and he will make your paths straight.'** - Proverbs 3:5-6(NIV)

There are some things that serve as pointers to destiny. They include but are not limited to:

   i) Prophecy
   ii) A call/divine encounter
   iii) Your natural gifts and Spiritual Gifts
   iv) Your body frame
   v) Challenges faced in the past
   vi) The lives and pains of others

I)   Prophecy

Sometimes people are foretold the kind of children they will give birth to and what they will do for God in their lifetime. Jesus was a perfect example of this. Apart from Him, the purpose of John was also revealed to his parents before he was born and it was later communicated to him.

In the Old Testament, Samson was a man whose birth was announced by an angel; his gender was mentioned and his mission on earth was equally made known. Not only that; his parents were instructed on how to bring him up.

> *'And there was a certain man of Zorah, of the family of the Danites, whose name was Manoah; and his wife was barren, and bare not. And the angel of the Lord appeared unto the woman, and said unto her, Behold now, thou art barren, and bearest not: but thou shalt conceive, and bear a son. Now therefore beware, I pray thee, and drink not wine nor strong drink, and eat not any unclean thing: for, lo, thou shalt conceive, and bear a son; and no razor shall come on his head: for the child shall be a Nazarite unto God from the womb: and he shall begin to deliver Israel out of the*

hand of the Philistines.' Judges 13:2-5. (KJV)
Carefully following the story of Samson in the Bible made us to realize that purpose can be thwarted. Because God said you would do great works for Him does not mean it will automatically get done. That is reserved for another chapter.

ii) A call/divine encounter

God calls out sometimes audibly to the vessel He uses. He tries and gets their attention and separates them for

> Carefully following the story of Samson in the Bible made us to realize that purpose can be thwarted.

a holy use. Moses and Paul of Tarsus are men who were called in like manner.

> *'And the angel of the Lord appeared unto him in a flame of fire out of the midst of a bush: and he looked, and, behold, the bush burned with fire, and the bush was not consumed. And Moses said, I will now turn aside, and see this great sight, why the bush is not burnt. And when the Lord saw that he turned aside to see, God called unto him out of the midst of the bush, and said, Moses, Moses. And he said, here am I. Now therefore, behold, the cry of the children of Israel is come unto me: and I have also seen the*

***oppression wherewith the Egyptians oppress
them. Come now therefore, and I will send thee
unto Pharaoh, that thou mayest bring forth my
people the children of Israel out of Egypt.'***
Exodus 3 vs 2-4, 9-10. (KJV)

This encounter with God marked a turning point in the
life of Moses and that was how he signed up in fulfilling
destiny. He became a deliverer through whom the
oppression of Egypt was broken over the Israelites. He
would have lived below his potential had it not been
that he was involved with that Divine encounter. The
journey to purpose starts when you know what needs
to get done!

After the ascension of Jesus, the church started
spreading and more people were added to the church.
Saul was breathing out threats against the church and
purposely went to the leading authority of the day to get
an arrest warrant to pick up the new converts and have
them tortured and killed. Unknown to him he had been
chosen by God to preach the gospel he was fighting
against. He didn't know until he discovered his purpose
in an unusual encounter.

***'And Saul, yet breathing out threatenings and
slaughter against the disciples of the Lord,
went unto the high priest, and desired of him
letters to Damascus to the synagogues, that if***

he found any of this way, whether they were men or women, he might bring them bound unto Jerusalem. And as he journeyed, he came near Damascus and suddenly there shined round about him a light from heaven. And he fell to the earth, and heard a voice saying unto him, Saul, Saul, why persecutest thou me? And he said, who art thou, Lord? And the Lord said, I am Jesus whom thou persecutest: it is hard for thee to kick against the pricks. And he trembling and astonished said, Lord, what wilt thou have me to do? And the Lord said unto him, arise, and go into the city, and it shall be

Unknown to him (Paul) he had been chosen by God to preach the gospel he was fighting against. He didn't know until he discovered his purpose in an unusual encounter.

told thee what thou must do.' Acts 9:1-6.

'But the Lord said unto him, Go thy way: for he is a chosen vessel unto me, to bear my name before the Gentiles, and kings, and the children of Israel.' Acts 9:15. (KJV)

His salvation was spectacular and the transformation that happened after that time was incredible. A man who was breathing persecution against the church later became a great voice for the gospel of the Lord Jesus

Christ. He wrote more books in the New Testament than the disciples that were handpicked and chosen directly by Jesus. Till date, he is still speaking to the church through his epistles; the letter he wrote to the churches!

iii)   Your natural gifts and Spiritual gifts

Another pointer to your destiny are your natural gifts; the things that you are naturally endowed with. Your gift may be compassion. As simple as that is, that is what a lot of businesses thrive on. There is something that God has put in you that looks so mundane with which you can affect your world positively; discover it! You have a talent, a gift, a passion that burns within you; with it you can rule the world. Make good use of it. Afer you are born again and are filled with the Holy Spirit, you are also usually endowed with spiritual gifts to help you fulfil your life's purpose.

iv)   Your stature/body frame

The body God has given you is the best He has prepared for your assignment. Whether you are short or tall can be a pointer to what you came here to do. It could be for sports or security purposes. It could be for other roles. You can decide to use your body frame for a noble cause. It all depends on you. Esther used her beauty to enter the king's palace and later as a queen saved her race. Delilah used her beauty and wits to pull down Samson

57

and destroyed his destiny; the choice is all yours. Long, short, tiny, bent or 'out of shape', you will do well to love your body. That is the jacket you will wear until you die. Don't wish you were someone else. Use the beauty accessories that complement your body frame and what you have will always be GORGEOUS.

> *'I praise you because I am fearfully and wonderfully made; Your works are wonderful, I know that full well'* -Psalms 139:14(NIV)

> *'Wherefore when he cometh into the world, he saith, sacrifice and offering thou wouldest not, but a body hast thou prepared me.'* Hebrews

The body God has given you is the best He has prepared for your assignment. Whether you are short or tall can be a pointer to what you came here to do.

10:5. (KJV

v)   **Challenges faced in the past**

> *Praise be to the God and Father of our Lord Jesus Christ, the Father of compassion and the God of all comfort, who comforts us in all our troubles, so that we can comfort those in any trouble with the comfort we ourselves receive from God.* -2Corinthians 1:3-4(NIV)

Your pain might end up as someone's pain; only if it is shared. What you have gone through and survived is what somebody is battling with now. God may allow you to go through an unpleasant situation so that you can become a voice that would heal their pains. The famous American televangelist Joyce Meyer narrated how her father used to abuse her sexually when she was young and how it affected her until she became born again. Her pain and how she overcame it gave hope to millions across the globe to see how they can let go of the past and embrace what God has prepared for their future.

vi)   The lives and pain of others

You might have a nudging in your heart that could lead you along a certain path. Many orphanages came into existence as a result of this. Many organizations have been established, many schools built just because somebody saw a need to ease the pain of others.

BEHIND THE SCENES

God will take time to train and refine His instruments. Often times, the trainings are not officially carried out. Because of this, a lot of people may not know that there is a training going on. God will cut off the excesses and put some things in place to ensure we effectively deliver when we get on set.

After being sold off into slavery, Joseph moved from Potiphar's house to the prison. In transit, he had the opportunity of sleeping with his master's wife but he never did. God was testing his heart. The master did not suffer any loss while he was in the house; with him, the question of integrity was settled. Later when he became the prime minister of Egypt he was able to freely forgive

Many organizations have been established, many schools built just because somebody saw a need to ease the pain of others.

his brothers who sold him off to slavery.

> **'He sent a man before them, even Joseph, who was sold for a servant: Whose feet they hurt with fetters: he was laid in iron until the time that his word came: the word of the Lord tried him. The king sent and loosed him; even the ruler of the people, and let him go free. He made him lord of his house, and ruler of all his substance.'**- Psalms 105:17-20(KJV)

It was actually the hand of God that led him to all the places he went to. God allowed him to pass through the furnace in preparation for the role he was born to take. What do you think would have happened to him if God didn't take him through the long process of Potiphar's house and the prison before showcasing him in Egypt? He probably would have been on a revenge mission and by so would fail to see the hand of God working things out in his favour. When his brothers became jittery after their father's death and thought he might avenge the evil they did to him, he assured them of their wellbeing. He realized that although his brothers meant it for evil; God used it to preserve the nations during famine.

Behind the scenes is where our flaws are laid out and polished. Peter denied Jesus but he later wrote a book in the New Testament. He missed it along the path but he quickly got up, dusted himself and went on to fulfil his purpose. David was referred to as a man after the heart of God. Does that mean he had it all straightened out with God? On the contrary, he slipped in his walk; he stumbled and fell flat on his face!

David stayed back when he should be at the battle field. As a result, he committed adultery with another man's wife and went a step further by ordering the husband of the woman to be killed in a gruesome manner! Yes, David fell down but he didn't stay down. He got up and went back to God in repentance. As a result, he got back on track and was able to fulfil his purpose.

Before David was chosen to lead the people of God he was taken from the sheep pen where he was taking care of the sheep. And he has this testimony at the end of his assignment that he led the people according to the integrity of his heart.

> *He chose David his servant and took him from the sheep pens; from tending the sheep he brought him to be the shepherd of his people Jacob, of Israel his inheritance. And David shepherded them with integrity of heart;'* Psalms 78:70-72(NIV)

Behind the scenes is where our flaws are laid out and polished.

THEY PLAYED THEIR ROLE

Jesus knew what He was born to do and that served as the guide to all that He did. The knowledge of being born for a purpose kept Him from allowing the people to make Him an earthly king. When you know the purpose for which you were brought here, that becomes the nucleus that you MUST concentrate all your passion, energy and time on.

> *'Then those men, when they had seen the miracle that Jesus did, said, This is of a truth that prophet that should come into the world. When Jesus therefore perceived that they*

62

would come and take him by force, to make him a king, he departed again into a mountain himself alone.' John 6:14-15.

'The thief cometh not, but for to steal, and to kill, and to destroy: I am come that they might have life, and that they might have it more abundantly.' John 10:10.

'He that committeth sin is of the devil for the devil sinneth from the beginning. For this purpose the Son of God was manifested, that he might destroy the works of the devil.' 1 John 3:8.

'At daybreak, Jesus went out to a solitary place. The people were looking for Him and when they came to where He was, they tried to keep Him from leaving them. But He said, "I must proclaim the good news of the kingdom of God to the other towns also, because that is why I was sent.' -Luke 4:42-43(NIV).

After Daniel located and understood what was to be done in the book, he successfully handled the administrative aspect of the royal kingdom of Babylon under three kings. He was relevant each and every time the kings were at a cross road and needed to make major decisions.

63

Esther was to preserve her race and she did.

Joseph was to keep nations alive in famine and he didn't disappoint God.

David, a man after God's heart led His people with integrity of heart and skilfulness of hands. He also lived up to his mandate. He did not fail God in his purpose.

Noah was to keep the entire human race alive after the flood. Despite the mockery and insults thrown at him, he did not stop until what God wanted was done. He followed the specific instructions laid out for him in constructing the ark.

Are you behind the scenes now being prepared by God for your role? It pays to let Him finish His work in you. After being tried you shall come forth shining like 'pure gold'.

Daniel located and understood what was to be done in the book, he successfully handled the administrative aspect of the royal kingdom of Babylon

OVERVIEW

Your assignment could be likened to a movie role and before you take up the task, God will take time to prepare you in advance. Sometimes He may allow us to go through unpleasant situations to form and develop our wings so that we can soar in our purpose as the eagle does.

REFLECTION

i)   Do you face challenges with courage or cringe before them? Do you aspire to travel along unfamiliar routes? You must learn how to watch the 'behind the scenes' of great artists. They will reveal how they missed their lines, forgot a key word or how they were encouraged to get in the right frame of mind for their role. Success doesn't just happen. Everybody who has attempted great things and succeeded failed earlier on in their attempt. Abraham Lincoln is one out of a sea of others.

YOU ARE PLAYING A LEAD ROLE

Everyone has inside of him a piece of good news. The good news is that you don't know how great you can be! How much you can love! What you can accomplish! And what your potential is!
- Anne Frank

YOU
ARE PLAYING
A LEAD ROLE

Minor' people have turned out playing major roles. More often than not, when God beckons people to undertake a certain task for Him they always turn it down. They try to escape and dodge the work. They feel they are not up to the task when they weigh the magnitude of the work against their capacity. The truth of the matter is if you can do it by your strength and with your own skills in spite of the weight of the assignment, then it really isn't God's work. Anything worthwhile, even in the secular, is always beyond what a single man can handle. A great assignment involves pooling resources and human skills together. No single man can achieve anything notable on his own; all alone.

God doesn't choose the 'able'. He prefers working with the people He can work on and equip. The people who have it all always end up making a mess of the job. They rely on their strength and see no need for God; and God cannot share His glory with any man. He is God all by Himself and needs no man to 'help' Him execute His project.

God has scripted a role for you and no matter how small and insignificant it seems, it fits somewhere in His overall design. What God has called you to do, can be done. Why am I so sure? He has given us enough promises in His word.

> *'Not that we are competent in ourselves to claim anything for ourselves, but our competence comes from God.'*
> -2 Corinthians 3:5(NIV)

> *'I can do all this through Him (Christ) who gives me strength.'* -Philippians 4:13(NIV)

God doesn't choose the 'able'. He prefers working with the people He can work on and equip.

The greater One lives on the inside of you! No matter how daunting the challenge is, you can overcome it. That is the spirit.

If God brought you to it, He will take you through it. If He called you to do it, His grace will be sufficiently supplied to you to enable you accomplish it. There is no amount of demand that you place on the grace of God that will make it run dry. It is always in abundance and will always be sufficient for any role you need to undertake.

> *'But he said to me, "My grace is sufficient for you, for my power is made perfect in weakness..."* 2 Corinthians 12:9(NIV)

WEAK VESSELS

Let's take a look at some people who felt they were not up to the task God gave them. They felt unqualified in one way or the other to make meaning out of the script He wrote for them. Their lives are a clear demonstration that when God calls, He supplies the grace needed to perfectly interpret your role no matter how daunting it seems.

1.   Moses

When God spoke to Moses through the burning bush, he was just eager to carefully watch the strange sight before him. He didn't know that he was being signed up for a role; a major role at that. Instead of being happy and embrace it, he took a long hard look at himself and carefully explained to God that he wasn't the choice candidate.

70

'Moses raised another objection to God: "Master, please, I don't talk well. I've never been good with words, neither before nor after you spoke to me. I stutter and stammer. God said, "And who do you think made the human mouth? And who makes some mute, some deaf, some sighted, some blind? Isn't it I, God? So, get going. I'll be right there with you—with your mouth! I'll be right there to teach you what to say." -Exodus 4:10-12 (The Message)

2. Gideon

When God wanted to save His people from the oppression of the invaders He thought of Gideon. Just like Moses he too was quick to point out to God why he couldn't fit into that role. Saving an entire nation from

> When God calls, He supplies the grace needed to perfectly interpret your role no matter how daunting it seems.

the oppression of the enemy looked like a mission impossible and Gideon wasn't ready to be a part of a failed project. So before he embarked on it, he tried to persuade God to look for a qualified vessel. Even the strong at heart do sometimes become fearful much less a man with a frail in his estimation of himself and his poor family background.

71

'The Lord turned to him and said, "Go in the strength you have and save Israel out of Midian's hand. Am I not sending you?" "Pardon me, my lord," Gideon replied, "but how can I save Israel? My clan is the weakest in Manasseh, and I am the least in my family. The Lord answered, "I will be with you, and you will strike down all the Midianites, leaving none alive." "- Judges 6:14-16(NIV)

I want you to notice that God promised to be with Gideon. That is the same assurance He gave Moses. The presence of God with you will enable you to perform any task He has assigned to you. The presence of God guarantees success. No matter what He is nudging your heart to do, get ready for His ever abiding presence to make it come to pass. The word of God says even the mountains melt like wax at the presence of the Lord! The hills skip like rams before Him. He is such a great God that cannot be intimidated by anything. Great waters are driven back when they see the awesome presence of Jehovah God.

Nothing compares to the presence of God. He is a mighty Man of war. He is strong and mighty. He is called the Lord of hosts. Anything that will hinder you or intimidate you must first of all scare God out of the way. If God promises to be with you, you can rest, assured that the victory has been won already. His presence guarantees success.

3.   Barak

Sometimes you need the presence of a personality that you feel is strong and capable to stand by you before you can fulfil your purpose. Barak told Deborah he wasn't going out in the battle against Sisera unless Deborah was ready to go with him. So bravery is not a question of gender. Men as well as women can feel intimidated when they consider the weight of their life's assignment and purpose. It is always a source of encouragement when there is somebody that you trust close by to cover your back in battle.

In fulfilling your purpose in life you may need to consciously enter into partnership with another person with a similar vision in order to play your role well. The word of God says 'iron sharpens iron.'

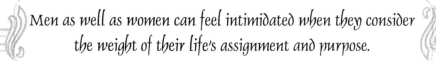

Men as well as women can feel intimidated when they consider the weight of their life's assignment and purpose.

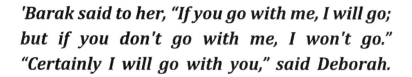

'Barak said to her, "If you go with me, I will go; but if you don't go with me, I won't go." "Certainly I will go with you," said Deborah.

73

"But because of the course you are taking, the honor will not be yours, for the Lord will deliver Sisera into the hands of a woman." So Deborah went with Barak to Kedesh- Judges 4:8-9(NIV)

4.   Jonah

When Jonah was given his role, he thought of nothing else but how to escape from it. He felt it was a very difficult mission to get it done. Reluctantly he eventually succumbed to God's will. Whatever God wants you to do for Him is dear to His heart and must not be taken with levity. There is nothing as glorifying to God as taking up His roles for our lives and run with quick steps to see that they are done.

'Now the word of the Lord came unto Jonah the son of Amittai, saying, Arise, go to Nineveh, that great city, and cry against it; for their wickedness is come up before me. But Jonah rose up to flee unto Tarshish from the presence of the Lord, and went down to Joppa; and he found a ship going to Tarshish: so he paid the fare thereof, and went down into it, to go with them unto Tarshish from the presence of the Lord.' Jonah 1:1-3. (KJV)

WEAKER VESSELS

Sometimes victory is wrought by insignificant weapons. The people whose lives we examined as 'weak vessels' were directly called by God and they felt

Sometimes victory is wrought by insignificant weapons.

they couldn't do it. The people that are going to be mentioned here never knew they were sent on assignment by God. They performed their roles without getting any 'official invitation'. God uses different strategies to call out to each of us our roles. While others will be busy for God conducting mighty crusades in the nations of the earth; others may be God's partners who are shielded from public notice.

A sword could win a battle; a smile might also be all that is needed to end a war. The ways of God are unpredictable. His methods cannot be limited. He uses the mighty as well as the lowly. But the bottom line is whether we receive the attention and accolades of men or not, we must rise up to the occasion, brace up for the task and run with our life's purpose.

Naaman's little maid (2 Kings 5:1-4)

As mighty as Naaman was, he needed the touch of God. Unknown to him the link to the source of that touch was right under his roof in the form of a little slave girl that attended to his household. The little girl did not know that she was in that house to play a greater role other than serving tables. Her suggestion made the huge difference that turned the life of Naaman around. She fulfilled her role in what might seem like a casual way. When we talk about purpose, it is often seen with an assignment that is gigantic and spans over years before it gets fulfilled. It doesn't always have to be like that; what is somebody's great miracle may be your *'casual'* assistance.

> *'Now Naaman, captain of the host of the king of Syria, was a great man with his master and honourable, because by him the Lord had given deliverance unto Syria. He was also a mighty man in valour, but he was a leper. And the Syrians had gone out by companies, and had brought away captive out of the land of Israel a little maid; and she waited on Naaman's wife. And she said unto her mistress, would God my lord were with the prophet that is in Samaria! For he would recover him of his leprosy. And one went in, and told his lord, saying, thus and thus said the maid that is of the land of Israel.'* 2 Kings 5:1-4. (KJV)

Sometimes, the lives we are designed to affect are not so

far from us. The 'cathedral' that God wants us to build could be a neighbour's troubled marriage, a teenager on drugs or a single mother juggling her demanding career with raising her kids. If we are not spiritually alive and sensitive we may wait endlessly for the Producer to beckon on us for the big roles while the real 'major' role is left unattended to.

Miriam, Moses' sister (Exodus 2:4, 7-8)

The sister of Moses was used by God to watch over him and hand him over to his foster mother. She didn't know she was playing any role at all. She felt she was just obeying her mother to watch over her little brother. She became a tool of preservation in the hands of God when Moses' life was in danger.

> *'And his sister stood afar off, to wit what would be done to him. Then said his sister to Pharaoh's daughter, Shall I go and call to thee a nurse of the Hebrew women, that she may nurse the child for thee? And Pharaoh's daughter said to her, go. And the maid went and called the child's mother.'*

What is somebody's great miracle may be your 'casual' assistance.

Exodus 2:4, 7-8.   (KJV)

THE HELP OF GOD

God cannot lie, if He promised His grace, He will supply it as at when needed. God can be relied on to deliver all of His promises to us. Every time you feel you can't start out and fulfil the role God has prepared for you, just take time to roll over His promises in your heart and faith will well up. Anytime you start and you want to quit, always remember that He said His grace is enough for you. At no point in your journey of purpose must you accept defeat. Why? Because God has promised to always stay true to your cause.

Why we can rely on God in fulfilling purpose?

The first reason is because He promised to. If He has chosen us to do something He will also give us the strength to get it done. His presence will be around us all the way. He owns the assignment and supplies the needed resources to get things done. God is not a liar. If He wants it done He will come through for you.

> *'God is not human, that He should lie, not a human being, that He should change His mind. Does He speak and then not act? Does He promise and not fulfil?'* Num. 23:19(NIV)

Secondly, God will always raise up helpers of destiny for His cause. When it was time to fight and Barak was afraid of going to battle, God raised up Deborah to assist him. When it was time for the children of Israel to come out of Egypt, Aaron was raised up to help Moses to get the job done. God's work in our hands will never lack God's men on our path!

Lastly, we can rely on God because He will take all the glory concerning our lives and He will ensure that no other person shares His glory with Him. That is why He has chosen the foolish things of the world to display His power through them.

God is not a liar. If He wants it done He will come through for you.

'God purposely chose what the world considers nonsense in order to shame the wise, and he chose what the world considers weak in order to shame the powerful. He chose what the world looks down on and despises and thinks is nothing, in order to destroy what the world thinks is important. This means that no one can boast in God's presence.' 1 Corinthians 1:27-29(GNT)

As far as God is concerned it is not how enormous the task you did is as to how faithful you were in playing your part when you came on set.

79

In Mathew 20, a parable is told about a man who went out at various times of the day to hire people to work in his vineyard. In contemporary language, we can see this man as a business owner (a site/field owner) who at various hours of the day went out to call people to work for him. He went to call people in the morning, at noon, in the evening and some others were still being hired at the time earlier labourers were about to get paid. Surprisingly enough, the man gave them equal wages. That's not fair! In Human Resources it doesn't follow the rules, but the man promised them the same wage.

So whether you came in the morning, afternoon or night makes no difference to God; all that matters is that you came on the scene and you played your part. He is generous in His wealth and it is His own decision to use and distribute it as He so pleases.

> *"'His master replied, 'Well done, good and faithful servant! You have been faithful with a few things; I will put you in charge of many things. Come and share your master's happiness!'.'* Mathew 25:23(NIV)

God rewards faithfulness, whether you played a major or minor role. That is enough to calm your fears and let you know you can do His bidding for your life. You can NEVER impress God with the magnitude of what you do but rather with the love in your heart that prompts you to do what pleases Him.

OVERVIEW

There is nothing you are doing for God that is small. Each task is huge in weight in the light of what He desires to get accomplished by your purpose.

REFLECTION

I)   Do you cringe into oblivion when you stand before others, thinking you are not as good as they are? The truth is that what others lack has been deposited in you, and what you lack is also in others. Find out where you belong and discover what others struggle with that you do so well. You are not inferior to anybody in worth and value.

ii)   What you are doing is important too; don't let anybody talk you into believing that your gift/talents/potential is of less value. You are playing a lead role.

iii)   Do you applaud others when they are performing at their peak without feeling jealous? Giants admire other giants; they don't pull them down.

ENEMIES
OF PURPOSE

You know that under pressure, your faith-life is forced into the open and shows its true colors. So don't try to get out of anything prematurely. Let it do its work so you become mature and well-developed, not deficient in any way. James 1:3,4. (The Message)

ENEMIES OF PURPOSE

There are things that are engaged in constant warfare with our destiny. They are eager and always ready to ensure we fail to fulfil our purpose. These enemies are numerous. They are the things that can trip you off and hinder you from fulfilling your destiny. If others in the past fought against them and overcame; so can we. The Bible even states that Jesus was in every way tempted as we are, but...He did not sin. He did not succumb. He was not pulled under. We can rise above every storm and do what God expects of us. In spite of the prevalent opposition we can get great things done. We can march on like brave soldiers and conquer our territories. We can overcome any and every obstacle.

OBSTACLES TO PURPOSE

1.   Sin

'Therefore, since we are surrounded by such a

***great cloud of witnesses, let us throw off
everything that hinders and the sin that so
easily entangles. And let us run with
perseverance the race marked out for us'***
Hebrews 12:1 (NIV) (Emphasis mine)

The first thing we have to contend with on our way to
fulfilling purpose is sin. Sin will pull you down on your
journey if you let it. That explains why the Bible says we
should lay aside every weight and the sin that besets.
The weight of sin will make it impossible for us to walk
at the pace God expects us to. Sin can drag anyone down,
making it impossible to fulfil one's role in life.

In another Bible passage, we are implored to flee every
appearance of evil. We must not take delight in living in
sin because we can never ever act our role while living
in sin.

*The first thing we have to contend with
on our way to fulfilling purpose is sin*

Joseph fled from sin (Potiphar's wife's seduction) and
was able to preserve his destiny. David allowed sin to
take control when he stayed back from war and chose to
commit adultery with Bathsheba and kill her husband.
Sin can pull anyone down in the mud. The moment you
try to get comfortable with 'little' sins, you will

eventually move on in enjoying the 'big' ones that will forever hold you in their claws.

The reason Joseph did not sleep with his boss' wife was not because people were not around; no. He could have slept with her and got away with it. In fact, pleasing her at that point in time would put him in her good books. The Bible recorded that he was alone in the house with her but he said 'how can I do this great wickedness and sin against God?' (Genesis 39:9-Paraphrased). In other words, there will be opportunities for compromise but the onus rests on you to say no. Saying no does not mean the sin you are tempted in at that point in time is not pleasurable or would bring immediate punishment; no. Your rejection of sin will be because you love God.

> *'If I regard iniquity in my heart, the Lord will not hear me...'* Psalm 66:18.

> *'Abstain from all appearance of evil.'* 1 Thessalonians 5:22.

> *'And it came to pass about this time, that Joseph went into the house to do his business and there was none of the men of the house there within. And she caught him by his garment, saying, lie with me: and he left his garment in her hand, and fled, and got him out.'* Genesis

39:11-12. (KJV)

Sexual immorality has pulled down great men. Samson lost hold of purpose because he laid his head on the laps of Delilah. Before Delilah there have been cases of other women who were in his life. When you live in sin, its pleasures will close your eyes to its destructive venom. Sin has pleasures. A verse in the book of proverbs says 'stolen water is sweet.' The Bible refers to the fleeting 'pleasures' of sin. We must not believe the lie of the world that sin is without consequences. It has stings; it has rewards.

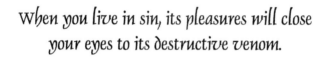

When you live in sin, its pleasures will close your eyes to its destructive venom.

'By faith Moses, when he had grown up, refused to be known as the son of Pharaoh's daughter. He chose to be mistreated along with the people of God rather than to enjoy the fleeting pleasures of sin.' Hebrews 11:24-25 (NIV)

Even if the pleasures of sin lasts a lifetime, it will still invite the wrath of God.

Sin has consequences. The word of God says the soul that sins shall die. Death may not mean instant separation from your physical body, but sin cuts people off from the presence of God. And once that happens, the essence of man is gone.

> *'The one who sins is the one who will die. The child will not share the guilt of the parent, nor will the parent share the guilt of the child. The righteousness of the righteous will be credited to them, and the wickedness of the wicked will be charged against them.'* Ezekiel 18:20 (NIV)

Gehazi lost it to greed. He was a servant to the man of God. When Naaman the leper came to the prophet of God and was cleansed of his leprosy, he offered to give the man of God gifts but he refused. Not long after, Gehazi, the servant ran after this great man and told him his master has sent him to collect the gifts earlier offered. Naaman joyfully obliged. Immediately he got back to his master, he told him that henceforth the leprosy of Naaman shall become his own and his children's children after him. Gehazi did not only truncate his own destiny; he pulled his generation down with him because of the sin of covetousness.

Judas was another man that sold his birth right because of thirty shekels of silver. He walked with Jesus and all he could look out for was an opportunity to betray him and enrich his pocket! The Bible recorded that he was in the habit of stealing money from the disciples' purse. As they went about healing the sick, preaching the good news, his interest lay in his pocket.

'But one of his disciples, Judas Iscariot, who was later to betray him, objected, "Why wasn't this perfume sold and the money given to the poor? It was worth a year's wages." He did not say this because he cared about the poor but because he was a thief; as keeper of the money bag, he used to help himself to what was put into it.' -John 12:4-6(NIV)

'And immediately, while he yet spake, cometh Judas, one of the twelve, and with him a great multitude with swords and staves, from the chief priests and the scribes and the elders. And he that betrayed him had given them a token, saying, whomsoever I shall kiss, that same is he; take him, and lead him away safely. And as soon as he was come, he goeth straightway to him, and saith, master, master; and kissed him. And they laid their hands on him, and took him.' Mark 14:43-45.

Gehazi did not only truncate his own destiny; he pulled his generation down with him because of the sin of covetousness.

'Men and brethren, this scripture must needs have been fulfilled, which the Holy Ghost by the

mouth of David spake before concerning Judas, which was guide to them that took Jesus. For he was numbered with us, and had obtained part of this ministry. Now this man purchased a field with the reward of iniquity; and falling headlong, he burst asunder in the midst, and all his bowels gushed out.' Acts 1:16-18. (KJV)

Judas started by taking whatever was put in the purse kept with him. He had been living in sin and thought he could get away with it. The greed that took hold of him led him to betray Jesus. Unfortunately the people who paid him refused to collect the money back after he realised what he did was wrong. As a result of the overwhelming guilt that drowned his soul, Judas Iscariot hung himself. What did he gain? He didn't even get to spend the money. Sin destroys. Its venom will always carry out its destructive purposes, no matter how appealing it appears.

2.   Pride

Another deadly obstacle is pride. When you play a role and you feel you are larger than life because of the fame and accolades that come your way, then you are setting yourself up for a great downfall. God is going to do great things in you and through you but you must never take the glory for anything that God has used you to achieve.

Learn to return all the glory to Him and don't have a bloated opinion of yourself and your abilities.

Pride pull's down

A great king built an empire, had a peaceful reign and was known the wold over. As he was walking on the rooftop of the palace one day, his heart became haughty and he said '***Is not this the great Babylon I have built as the royal residence, by my mighty power and for the glory of my majesty?'*** Daniel 4:30.

I want you to notice two things from his speech. The kingdom he built became great. That means in the context of this book he was able to play a lead role that became a hit. So in his own foolish conclusion, all that was achieved by his personal power and honour of his name. He failed to acknowledge God in his achievement. Anything you achieve is for God. He gives you the power; the enablement to get things done and it was in

Any role you played must be interpreted for the honour of His majesty and not yours.

His plan to have it done through you for the splendour and honour of His majesty. You are a vessel unto honour. Any role you played must be interpreted for the honour of His majesty and not yours. All the glory belongs to God.

91

'Not to us, Lord, not to us but to Your name be the glory, because of Your love and faithfulness' Psalms 115:1(NIV)

God is a jealous God and He will never share His glory with ANYONE. Anyone or anything that takes the place of God is an idol. When your heart becomes lifted up and haughty, you are indirectly saying you are self-sufficient and have no need of God. That is the first step towards destruction.

'Pride goes before destruction, a haughty spirit before a fall.' Proverbs 16:18(NIV)
'...God opposes the proud but shows favour to the humble..' 1 Peter 5:5(NIV)

There is grace and it is available only for those who are humble. I think that is what made it possible for David to have a comeback. When he stumbled, he retraced his steps and came back to God.

When the heart of Nebuchadnezzar was lifted up in pride, God sent him to the forest to live amongst animals for seven years until he came back to his senses. Read this story in the Book of Daniel chapter 4:28-34.

It is better for you to humble yourself and be clothed with humility. It is beautiful to be humble. Any gift you have that is bringing you fame, money or pleasure should not make you lift up your heart high against God. If you do that, you start giving out an offensive smell. On the other hand, if you are humble, the humility coming from the perfect interpretation of your role will make you more beautiful than how you really are.

Only humble people can receive grace from God. When the grace of God is upon your life it will make it easy for you to fulfil purpose. Lack of humility will cause friction for you and it will be like an engine running short on oil.

3.   Distraction

On the journey of purpose, you must always keep your eyes on your script and the role you are here to play.

It is beautiful to be humble... Only humble people can receive grace from God.

That is the guide; the map that will lead you to the place designed for you. You were not born to be everything-in the popular slogan, you are not a 'jack of all trade'. You can't take up the role of every other actor on the cast. You are not made for every role, rather you have a unique role to play. No matter how appealing other people's roles may seem, learn from them, celebrate them but don't wish you were playing their role. Magnify your office. Do your best and play your role well.

Before the public manifestation of Jesus a lot of people felt that John was the Messiah that was promised to the nation of Israel. They wanted to confirm this from him so that they could accord him the respect of that office. He didn't mince words but stated his role in regards to the coming of the Messiah. He told them that he was only a voice and that he only came to prepare the way for Him.

If John was not clear about his life's purpose and mission he would have succumbed to the desire of the people to place him where he didn't belong. You must be satisfied with what you are here to do. When you focus on your life's purpose you will learn all there is to that role and deliver excellently. The moment you begin to lose concentration and look here and there, fulfilling your role will become difficult.

Let your script consume your time and your passion. Let it be all you think about, plan about and the only picture that you see and concentrate on. Don't try to be who God has not called you to be. Don't try to play the role that God didn't ascribe to you. People who think they know more about your script will come with their various suggestions, opportunities to divert, promises attached to letting go of your role, but you must tenaciously stay on your path and refuse to swerve.

You're blessed when you stay on course,
walking steadily on the road revealed by God.
You're blessed when you follow His directions,
doing your best to find Him.
That's right you don't go off on your own; you
walk straight along the road He set.
-Psalms 119:1-3(The Message)

4. Character flaws

A man who rules over his spirit is more powerful than a man who can carry the gate of a city. The ability to develop your character is a great asset. Being able to rule over your appetite cannot be over emphasized. Samson had the power to kill men in their thousands but he couldn't control his affection for women. Delilah

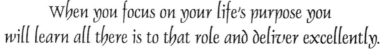

When you focus on your life's purpose you will learn all there is to that role and deliver excellently.

was not the first woman he fell in love with. He just loved women and couldn't control his urge for having more and more of them.

Whatever rules over you is your master. You must learn to discipline yourself and walk in the consciousness of your role. You must tell yourself that nothing is going to hinder you from performing your duty. The devil has baits that he throws at the children of God from time to time. The Bible says we shouldn't be ignorant of his devices. He has plans that are carefully schemed out and waiting for the perfect time to execute them. We must be very alert and watchful.

We need to know that whatever we do now will be magnified when we get to the peak of wherever God is taking us. That is why we must consciously work on ourselves and prepare for where God is taking us to. You must develop the character that is going to support the role we are going to play. If you are acting as a king, you sure must display royalty. If you are leading God's people you must have the passion for men and show empathy or else you will be leading people with an iron rod.

Anywhere God has placed you is for you to effect a positive change and not for your selfish gain; it is to bring glory to Him. You must 'wear' the personality of the role you are taking. If you are called into the five-fold ministry please show Christ to the world. If you are called into the medical field you must be willing to care for people who are ill with an empathetic and genuine desire to see them bounce back to good health.

The role you are playing determines the costume you will wear for your role. You can't eat or do anything that will not enable you to perform well. If you have been called to take care of the aged, you must be very tolerant and understand their views. If God has called you to operate in this area you need to know that you must be very friendly. You must consciously work on yourself to be friendly at all times. If you have received a mandate, from God to make a change in the educational sector you must put academic excellence above monetary gain. Any field of endeavour that God has prepared for you must be seen as something very sacred. You must put pleasing God and service to humanity first.

> ***Whatever you do, work at it with all your heart, as working for the Lord, not for human masters*** Colossians 3:23-NIV

Your character will either make or mar you. Any monster you fail to put to death now will raise its ugly head and pull you down when you get on set. It is easier

 You must 'wear' the personality of the role you are taking.

to straighten out your character when you are still behind the scene. The flaws you don't work on now will be magnified when you get to the peak of where God has placed you.

The Bible exhorts us to contend for the faith. That means that there are things that will try to stand on our path to fulfilling purpose. It is our duty to fight against all the things that try to get in our way. The issue of purpose involves fighting to stay on track and fighting to get it right. When David missed it in his walk with God he quickly retraced his steps and went to Him in repentance. That was why he was able to have this testimony written about him in the book of Acts

> *'For David, after he had served his own generation by the will of God, fell on sleep...'* Acts 13:36.

David had this testimony that he served his own generation according to the will of God. He did what God created him to do in his own time. This is your own time; your own generation; how are you serving?

At the end of our journey in life, may we be able to say like Paul 'I have fought the good fight, I have finished the race, and I have kept the faith...' (2 Timothy 4:7)NIV.

It is when you finish your race that you can get a reward. Don't try to impress anybody or run another man's race. Face your destiny with a tenacity to finish well. It is worth the fight!

OVERVIEW

There are things that trip people up on the road to destiny. They are things that shift people's eyes from the main thing and hinder them from getting the prize. Flee from them.

REFLECTION

I)   Are you easily distracted when you undertake tasks?

ii) Do you acknowledge that you have limitations and can fall down? The moment you feel you can never fall; you are already setting yourself up for a fall. The strongest of men struggle with issues. Being sincere in the appraisal of your strength is a great help.

iii) There are other people who are strong where you are weak. Networking helps.

MEN
OF SIMILAR
SCRIPTS

..."Let Reuben live and not die,
nor his people be few."(Deut. 33:6)

MEN OF SIMILAR SCRIPTS

The place you are going in life is different from where another person is heading for. You can't walk with everybody on your journey in life; that is simply because you may be heading in opposite directions. That is why the course of the journey of purpose may sometimes be charted through a lonely path.

However, there are people that God has designed to be part of your journey here on earth. They have been stationed on different paths of your journey to make an input that will help you finish 'your race'. They have a role to play alongside yours and they have an input to make in your life.

No man, no matter how strong, has ever singlehandedly fulfilled the counsel of God without other people planted along his path. You must realize that you need other people. You can't do it all alone.

The people that God has ordained for you will come in at

different points of your life. Their respective entry point will differ. They will be there to cheer you on, support you and hold the ladder while you are climbing. The different scenes you are going to feature in are going to require other people 'yoked' with you.

When Moses was about to die, he called the twelve tribes and prayed for them. One of the prayers he prayed for them is that God will bring them to their people and that their people will not be few. Two prayers in one; may God bring you to your people and may your people not be few. I think he was in the best

No man, no matter how strong, has ever singlehandedly fulfilled the counsel of God without other people planted along his path.

position to pray this prayer for the tribe of Reuben and Judah. During his time, he had men who were stationed to protect his cause right from the time he was born, through the time he fulfilled his purpose and died.

>   *'...nor his men be few... bring him unto his people...'* Deut. 33:6, 7.

When Moses was born, the king ordered that all the male children born to the Israelites be killed. His first point of help was when there was a need for him to either get killed or be spared. The first 'men' that God used to preserve him were the midwives. God put it in their hearts to deal tenderly with the Hebrew women. Shiphrah and Puah feared God and refused to kill all the male children born to the Israelites at the time when the king's order was fierce. They let them live. They were playing a role alongside Moses; but they didn't know. God has ordained that at that point in time, they will be used of Him to keep Moses alive for His purpose. That was the first point of entry for the helpers of his destiny.

The life of a man is filled with men of similar scripts; it is just that they come in varying degrees. The time they will come into your life and how long they stay will depend on their mission. There are some people that have been planted on your journey to make a huge impact in very subtle ways. The midwives started the journey of liberating the people of God. In His master plan they were divinely placed by God in the medical field to preserve a nation. But...they never could have known that it was beyond the call of duty not to have killed Moses alongside other male children. They didn't even think along the line of disobeying the king. They just felt they should preserve the male children without knowing they were actually playing a role.

Some of the people that God used in preserving you on the journey of purpose are men that you can't trace and say 'thank you' to.

The midwives did it for Moses before he even knew who he was as a person. Most of the time, such people could really have played their part before you start acting your role. Exodus 1:13-17

Moses went further in playing his role with men of similar scripts when his sister stepped in on the stage with him. After a period of time his mother could no longer keep him. She decided to let go of him when she could no longer hide him from impending danger. She put baby Moses in a cot she constructed for him and placed him beside a river. Her sister stood close by to see what would befall him.

Unknown to the daughter of Pharaoh, she was the next

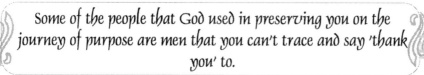

Some of the people that God used in preserving you on the journey of purpose are men that you can't trace and say 'thank you' to.

person assigned to act in line with Moses. She was also playing a major role in his life. At that point in time, the God who sees and knows ahead of time ordered her steps to go to the river side to bathe. Why would she go at that point in time? Why not some other time? In the process, she discovered a baby along the bank of the river. She knew quite alright that it was one of the children of the Israelites, yet she decided to adopt him.

The men that God have planned for your destiny do not necessarily have to love you or be of the same race or class with you. As far as they are part of your script, they will play along.

God is awesome. His word says 'when the way of a man pleases the Lord, He makes even his enemies to be at peace with him!' That was true in the case of Moses. God used the same king that wanted to eliminate him to raise him. Not only that, his mother was paid for nursing him. The ways of God are beyond what we can fathom.

The men that God have planned for your destiny do not necessarily have to love you or be of the same race or class with you.

Bring him to his people and let not his men be few! God brought Moses to his people and the men He used were not few.

'In the Lord's hand the king's heart is a stream of water that he channels toward all who please him.' Proverbs 21:1(NIV)

God turned the heart of Pharaoh to work in Moses' favour. He carefully stationed people along his path to work out His plan for His people.

Moses was a man who enjoyed the help of God all the way. From birth till the time he discovered his essence of being born and carrying out his assignment, he was never without men who had similar scripts as himself.

There was a time when he was involved in warfare with the Amalekites. When he was fighting with them, Aaron and Hur went up to the mountain with him. It was discovered that every time his hands were raised up the Israelites were winning, but whenever his hands went down the Amalekites prevailed against the people of God. These two men decided to keep him in a winning posture and put stones under his hands. That is what the people that God has ordained for your life will do for you. They will hold your hands up. The men with similar

 The men with similar scripts will never pull you down. They will ensure they give their all

scripts will never pull you down. They will ensure they give their all; even their lives, if need be, in order to see you fulfil purpose. Men of similar scripts could be rightly called the 'helpers of your destiny'. They are sent by God to assist you in your assignment.

'So Joshua did as Moses had said to him, and fought with Amalek: and Moses, Aaron, and Hur went up to the top of the hill. And it came to

pass, when Moses held up his hand, that Israel prevailed: and when he let down his hand, Amalek prevailed. But Moses' hands were heavy; and they took a stone, and put it under him, and he sat thereon; and Aaron and Hur stayed up his hands, the one on the one side, and the other on the other side; and his hands were steady until the going down of the sun. And Joshua discomfited Amalek and his people with the edge of the sword. And the Lord said unto Moses, write this for a memorial in a book, and rehearse it in the ears of Joshua for I will utterly put out the remembrance of Amalek from under heaven.' Exodus 17:10-14.

The men that God has prepared for this assignments are not ready to receive accolades or share in His glory; they just want the job done. They just want you to excel where God has placed you. The men of similar scripts are the people that share your vision with you. They believe in your God-given mission. They will support you with their resources, godly counsel, their strength and prayers and may surrender their lives in the process. They are your own people. I pray that such men will not be few in your life.

Aaron did not stop with holding up the hands of Moses. He acted alongside this vessel ordained by God to deliver his people from the oppression of Egypt. He was there all the way.

Another person that played a positive role in the life of Moses was Jethro; his father-in-law. He gave him godly

Some people will be part of your life and without being told you will know that they are a big fat plus to your destiny.

counsel so that he could have the energy to pour into the assignment given to him instead of burning his energy to settle disputes. Jethro helped Moses a great deal. Because of his advice, his son-in-law was able to fight against distraction and focus his energy on the main thing.

Some people will be part of your life and without being told you will know that they are a big fat plus to your destiny. Others will come and you will know that you have been unequally yoked. Allowing such people stay will lead to them pulling you down, sapping you of your energy and add nothing of value to you. In ancient times, oxen of equal weight and strength were yoked together for agricultural purposes. By so doing, the weight of the work is equally shared amongst them. In order to get the most of them they must have the same vision and walk in the same direction, if these things are not in place they will do more harm than good and the essence of coming together would be defeated. This is true for every covenant relationship especially marriage.

Mary was pregnant before marriage (though through the Power of the Holy Spirit) and she must have been afraid and a bit ashamed. That could be because her carefully planned life was altered. Elizabeth had her baby when she was past age of fertility and she was ecstatic. Guess what, they were both acting similar roles and they interconnected.

When Mary came in contact with Elizabeth, something within them connected. They knew they were meant to be together for that season. The respective seeds they were carrying had something to give to each other. Elizabeth was carrying John the forerunner of Jesus Christ the Saviour that Mary was carrying. There will be a link between you and your men with similar scripts. When you come in contact with them, please make the most of that golden opportunity. Sometimes, God will allow you to know and meet the people that He has destined to play alongside with you. When you meet such people, create time to draw out virtue from them.

The Bible records that when Mary's greeting came to

Elizabeth, she was immediately filled with the Holy Spirit. That is the meeting point! The power needed for her to do what she was meant to do was deposited in her at that moment. She referred to Mary as 'the mother of my Lord.' She knew that Mary was not just a little cousin, family or a friend. She recognized that fact that this was beyond a casual relationship between the two of them. Sometimes, the people that will play major roles in your life are people that are very close to you. It now behoves you to be careful not to abuse intimacy and take their relationship for granted. Doing that will make it difficult for you to draw out the virtue you need to play your lead role. The people you are playing with may not be as 'mature', talented or of the same disposition as you are, but the bottom line is that God has placed you there at that point in time to draw out virtue for that stage of your life.

> Sometimes, the people that will play major roles in your life are people that are very close to you. It now behoves you to be careful not to abuse intimacy

'And Mary arose in those days, and went into the hill country with haste, into a city of Juda; and entered into the house of Zacharias, and saluted Elisabeth. And it came to pass, that, when Elisabeth heard the salutation of Mary, the babe leaped in her womb; and Elisabeth

111

was filled with the Holy Ghost: and she spake out with a loud voice, and said, blessed art thou among women, and blessed is the fruit of thy womb. And whence is this to me, that the mother of my Lord should come to me? For, lo, as soon as the voice of thy salutation sounded in mine ears, the babe leaped in my womb for joy.' Luke 1:39-44.

Don't waste any relationship that is God-ordained. Relationships are very vital in getting you to where God has prepared for you. When you come in contact with the men that have been positioned in your life, look at their script alongside yours and see how they are interwoven. It makes for good dialogue. When two people are featuring in a production and they refuse to rehearse together, there is no way they can be in sync when they get on stage. There is something called fusion. It can only occur when you take time to embrace the things the other person is bringing to the table and how you can add yours to it to fulfil a higher calling. The other person has something tangible to offer your destiny. At the end of his life the bible says this concerning him:

'Thus David the son of Jesse reigned over all Israel. And the time that he reigned over Israel was forty years; seven years reigned he in

Hebron, and thirty and three years reigned he in Jerusalem. And he died in a good old age, full of days, riches, and honour and Solomon his son reigned in his stead.' 1 Chronicles 29:26-28.

David was referred to as a man after God's Heart. He was a great king. All that he did was not accomplished single-handedly.

The Bible recorded that he died in a good old age, full of days, riches and honour. What happened before he

Don't waste any relationship that is God-ordained.

became the king? What were his struggles? Who are the people that played their roles along with him? David started as a shepherd. He was left to do the job that nobody at home was eager and willing to do at all. He was used to being alone with the sheep; he fed them and ensured their welfare. On so many occasions when they were attacked by ferocious animals, David ran after the wild animals, killed them and rescued his own.

When Samuel was sent by God to their house to anoint the new king for Israel, nobody thought David was unqualified. They must have felt he was of no significance or qualified for such important matters.

What they failed to realize was that when God calls a man He qualifies him for any role he's been called to play.

God had prepared men- people that would make it possible for him to get to the height meant for him to fulfil His counsel. The journey to the throne was far from easy. He was hunted like an animal; King Saul was ready to kill him at all cost... in spite of all his ordeals God led him to the throne in His own time.

Saul missed it in his duties when it was time for the kingdom to be turned over to David. But after God rejected him he didn't take him off the scene immediately. He was still the king of Israel. It was during the time he was there as an interim king that Goliath came to defy the army of Israel. David knew that at the right time, God would place him where he rightfully belonged. God helped him by planting so many people on his path.

You can never predict God. He sometimes uses people that should fight our destiny to help us in fulfilling our purpose on earth. Just as He used King Pharaoh to nurture one of the Hebrew male children he wanted dead. He also used Jonathan (a rightful heir to the throne) to ensure that David got there. He somehow knew that the kingdom had been taken from his father and transferred to David. Immediately David killed Goliath, the entire nation showed their preference for him above King Saul. Jonathan knew that following all human protocol he should be the next king in Israel. But he also knew that the kingdom has been taken from his father and transferred to David.

The people that God has prepared for your destiny will have compassion on you. The Bible records that the soul of Jonathan was knit with the soul of David. There was a bond; a link in the deepest part of their beings. Jonathan loved him like his own soul; as a result, they cut a covenant. When you cut a covenant with somebody, it means you are entering into the deepest level of commitment with them. It is beyond the ordinary surface level of friendship. It is noteworthy to see how they went about it.

A covenant is a solemn oath entered into by at least two people. It could extend beyond two people. The person who initiated the covenant is the covenant initiator while the person with whom the covenant is cut is

You can never predict God. He sometimes uses people that should fight our destiny to help us in fulfilling our purpose on earth.

known as the covenant responder. There is a witness, a person who stands between the initiator and the responder. There are terms and conditions of the covenant. When two people come into a covenant they are simply forming an alliance - a league. What they are saying is that they will join their strength together during crises and fight a common enemy. The enemy of one automatically becomes the enemy of the other.

In a covenant, there are symbols used to explain deeper truths about what is being done. There are a lot of things used to cut a covenant. Jonathan stripped himself of the robe he had on. That means he was ready from that moment on to cover him. A robe; a garment covers the user from being naked. When you are in a covenant, you must ensure that the person you are cutting the covenant with must not be exposed while you have a robe around you. It is that deep. In a covenant, it is all about the welfare of the other person.

Jonathan didn't stop there; he went further to give David his sword and his bow! What he was saying in essence was that all the weapons with which he protects himself are now for the safety of the future king of Israel. How could a man do that? Why would he give so much support to a man that was going to take his place and hinder him from becoming king? It was because he knew that God had transferred it from his father to David and he was ready to comply. If it was necessary, Jonathan was willing to give his life in exchange for David to ensure he was crowned king. May God raise men to protect your cause and ensure that the will of God for your life is done.

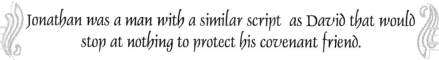

Jonathan was a man with a similar script as David that would stop at nothing to protect his covenant friend.

On so many occasions King Saul planned to kill David but Jonathan was always there to free his legs from every trap set for him. How could David have escaped being pinned to the wall by King Saul or survived being murdered had not God prepared Jonathan to defend his cause? Jonathan was a man with a similar script as David that would stop at nothing to protect his covenant friend.

> *'Now Hiram king of Tyre sent envoys to David, along with cedar logs and carpenters and stonemasons, and they built a palace for David.'* 2 Samuel 5:11. (NIV)

> *'Now these are they that came to David to Ziklag, while he yet kept himself close because of Saul the son of Kish: and they were among the mighty men, helpers of the war. They were armed with bows, and could use both the right*

hand and the left in hurling stones and shooting arrows out of a bow, even of Saul's brethren of Benjamin.' 1 Chronicles 12:1-2. (KJV)

'They helped David against raiding bands, for all of them were brave warriors, and they were commanders in his army. Day after day men came to help David, until he had a great army, like the army of God...' 1 Chronicles 12:21-22(NIV)

'These also are the chief of the mighty men whom David had, who strengthened themselves with him in his kingdom, and with all Israel, to make him king, according to the word of the LORD concerning Israel. And this is the number of the mighty men whom David had...' 1 Chronicles 11:10-11. (KJV)

According to the scriptures above, there were men who stood up for the cause of David. All of them came for just one singular purpose; to turn the kingdom to David according to what God had ordained.

Hiram king of Tyre sent men and resources to David to build a house for him.

The three mighty men went at the risk of losing their lives to get water for David. They broke through the host of the Philistines; the enemy's camp to fetch water for David to quench his thirst. 1 Chronicles 11:10-17.

David had this written concerning him that men came unto him day by day to help him until they became great, like a great army! That is the prayer Moses prayed. That men will rise up for your cause and that they will not be few. You need men of similar scripts on the road to fulfilling your God ordained purpose.

David had this written concerning him that men came unto him day by day to help him until they became great, like a great army!

This chapter will not be complete without making mention of how Jesus Christ fulfilled His purpose with men of similar script in His life and ministry. John the Baptist came and prepared the ground for His ministry. During His time of walking around healing the sick and turning people to the kingdom of God, the Bible recorded some women who contributed to the success of the work.

'And it came to pass afterward, that he went throughout every city and village, preaching and showing the glad tidings of the kingdom of

God and the twelve were with him, and certain women, which had been healed of evil spirits and infirmities, Mary called Magdalene, out of whom went seven devils, and Joanna the wife of Chuza Herod's steward, and Susanna, and many others, which ministered unto him of their substance.' Luke 8:1-3. (KJV)

These women mentioned in the scripture above gave to the cause of the gospel out of their substance. The work was able to move on and reach out to people in several places because some people committed themselves to giving. That was all that was said concerning them.

So in all, you will notice that people with similar scripts came before Jesus was born, prepared the ground for Him and the flow didn't stop like that. While he was actively involved with the work He came to do, some people also fulfilled their own roles alongside His ministry. After 'leaving' the scene, the play still goes on. Today, men throughout the world are still finding where they belong and fitting in.

No man is placed in your life by mistake. You must see the hands of God in planting people around you. However, God has given you the sole responsibility of choosing some people that you will work with. When it comes to walking with such people, you must agree to walk together. Like I said earlier in this book, when you are unequally yoked it will sap you of your energy and make it impossible for you to get the job that has been assigned to you done.

No man is placed in your life by mistake. You must see the hands of God in planting people around you.

One of the people that will greatly assist you on the journey of destiny is your spouse. You must therefore, prayerfully and carefully select who your soul mate will be. You can't afford to jeopardize your life's assignment because you want to please yourself. Your destiny could be marred by the choices you make in relationships.

> **'Be not deceived, evil communications corrupt good manners.'** 1 Corinthians 15:33(KJV)

Not only that, you must also know that God has entrusted you with the destiny of some people. If you have been given the grace to be a parent, please play your role very well as it will affect the lives and destinies of the children that God has committed to your care.

OVERVIEW

Your God-given assignment will involve other people that God has ordained to contribute their quota to it. You will do well to discover them and give room for synergy. There is multiplicity of effects when such people are a part of God's bigger vision concerning you.

REFLECTION

I)   The Bible says 'a friendly man must show himself friendly'. How friendly are you? Are you willing to have people in your circle or you prefer having your own space?

ii)   An African proverb says 'snakes are easily killed because they don't walk in groups'. There is power in synergy. God has intertwined the success of your purpose to the purpose of others. Learn how to cultivate and sustain meaningful relationships.

iii)   Because others have used you and taken advantage of you in the past doesn't mean everybody on earth is like that. Good people still abound! God will send them to your life from time to time. When they come, celebrate them and allow them to fulfill their role before they move on.

PURPOSE
AND SEASONS

*Yesterday's the past, tomorrow's
the future, but today is a gift.
That's why it's called the present.*
-Bil Keane

PURPOSE
AND SEASONS

Tick, tick, says the time
Yesterday 'twas 24 hours
Today it's same 24 hours
Tomorrow not an extra hour
Round the globe same tick, tick, says the clock
Nobody's going to get more hours
Not an extra minute for a thousand pleas
Not even an additional second for the mightiest king
Not a second less for the poorest of slaves
Every soul's got equal share
Tickling each day
When the sun wakes up the
clock would have woken earlier
When it rests it's not going to rest
As it ticks so do our days slip quietly
Into eternity they fly
Bearing on their wings our deeds

The psalmist said *'...teach us to number our days, that we may apply our hearts unto wisdom.'* – (Psalms. 90:12).

Our assignments in life and the essence of our being; the

fulfilment of our purpose or otherwise is carefully wrapped up in how well we make use of our days. As each day passes, never to return, the opportunities to fulfil our purpose also pass before us. Our lives are broken into times and seasons. There is a season to fulfil our purpose and this season falls within a time frame.

Just as we were born on a certain day, it is also guaranteed that we will die one day. Our date of birth, place of birth, and birth parents are not of great importance. The most important thing is for us to fulfil our purpose here on earth before we take a bow. The days stuck in between the date of birth and the dates of death are what we should guard jealously. Once a day is gone it can never be recalled. That is why the Psalmist

The most important thing is for us to fulfil our purpose here on earth before we take a bow.

prayed for God to teach us to number (not count) our days; so that we can apply our hearts unto wisdom. It is the wisdom of how to appropriately use our days (time) that we should ask from God. It takes having insight and the wisdom of God to make the best use of each of our days.

The sequence of what we were born to do will roll like a tape in different seasons of our lives. Our purpose will unfold in stages and we must not be slack when they do. Just as the preacher says in Ecclesiastes 3:1: **'There is**

125

time for everything, and a season for every activity under the heavens.' (NIV)

When we have the knowledge of how precious times and seasons are, we will embrace each day and run with joy to ensure that what has been fixed for that day gets done. We will also be careful to prevent running ahead of time not to do today what is meant for tomorrow. In God's timetable there is something called 'the fullness of time.' It is that time that heaven has ordained for a specific assignment to be carried out. Timing is very crucial to our purpose on earth. If we fail to complete the process that God has for us per time we will end up being of less use.

'... Ephraim is a cake not turned.' Hosea 7:8(KJV). A cake not turned is uncooked on one side. Its purpose has been thwarted. The same will apply to us if we don't allow God to finish His work in us. We must not run out of the prep room. We must tarry in His presence until we are fully refined, transformed and made ready for the Master's use. We will commit blunders if we don't allow Him to finish the work He has purposed in us.

The process through which a larva becomes a butterfly is gradual and systematic. The larva goes through different stages. Each of the stages has something significant to contribute to the overall development of the end result; a beautiful butterfly. If a stage is omitted the insect being formed will die prematurely; on the other hand if all the processes are duly observed, a lovely insect will emerge after the tedious struggle.

There are lessons that God has prepared us to learn in order to prepare us for the place of our assignment. Each of them will expose us to varying degrees of pain and struggle, but we can trust God who has assured us that all things will work out together for our good.

Moses knew while he was living in Pharaoh's palace that God was training him to deliver His people from the oppression of Egypt. But before the appointed time, he tried to truncate a phase of the metamorphosis stage. Before the appointed time for manifestation, Moses went to the field one day and saw an Israelite and an Egyptian fighting. He looked to his left and right and went ahead to hit the Egyptian thus killing him in the process. He quickly buried him in the sand and went back to the palace. Not quite long after, he saw two Israelites fighting. He offered to settle the fight amicably, but one of them was quick to tell him not to kill him the way he killed the Egyptian. That was the beginning of his refuge in a strange land. He fled when

In God's timetable there is something called 'the fullness of time.' It is that time that heaven has ordained for a specific assignment to be carried out.

he realized that the matter was already in the public domain.

While he was at the back of the desert, God was able to break him and mould him into what He desired. If he had continued killing the Egyptians in that fashion, he would have been doing God's work in the strength of his flesh and according to his own timing. The prophecy that went ahead of the children of Israel clearly stated the number of years the Israelites would be in bondage before they are delivered and restored to Canaan. There was timing involved; they would be slaves for a certain number of years and when the fullness of time comes, they would be restored back to their land. (Gen.15:13-16)

When Moses tried to do it ahead of time God had to keep him elsewhere so that he would be able to execute his life's purpose in the season that God has prepared fit according to His eternal plan. By that singular act he made the children of Israel spend extra thirty years in a strange land.

Timing and purpose are intertwined. When you take one out, the other becomes lame. A cake unturned is good for nothing and has defeated the purpose for which it was intended.

In fulfilling your purpose, don't try to outsmart God. Allow Him to finish His work in you so that you can bring Him glory by achieving His eternal counsel. Teach us to number our days...so that we can apply our hearts unto wisdom.

'And it came to pass in those days, when Moses was grown, that he went out unto his brethren, and looked on their burdens and he spied an Egyptian smiting an Hebrew, one of his brethren. And he looked this way and that way, and when he saw that there was no man, he slew the Egyptian, and hid him in the sand. And when he went out the second day, behold, two men of the Hebrews strove together: and he said to him that did the wrong, wherefore smitest thou thy fellow? And he said, who made thee a prince and a judge over us? Intendest thou to kill me, as thou killedst the Egyptian? And Moses feared, and said, surely this thing is known. Now when Pharaoh heard this thing, he sought to slay Moses. But Moses fled from the face of Pharaoh, and dwelt in the land of Midian.' Exodus 2:11-15. (KJV)

There's a time to go to war and there's a time to divide the spoils of war. Gehazi lost out on purpose because he

In fulfilling your purpose, don't try to outsmart God. Allow Him to finish His work in you...

didn't understand timing in purpose. It is not in the plan of God to have people work for Him without rewarding them. He said in His word that He is not unjust to forget our labour of love. When you walk with Him or work for Him He will assuredly reward you.

129

Gehazi was serving under Elisha and he should have been wise enough to closely follow his steps. His master could have demanded for silver and gold from Naaman and he would have gladly given them to him. In fact he constrained him to take gifts but Elisha blatantly refused. Gehazi saw an opportunity to extort money from Naaman. What he failed to realize is the fact that there is a time to accept gifts, and there is a time to refrain from taking gifts. If he waited for the perfect time, he would have remained relevant in the ministry where God had called him and God would have given him the wages due to his commitment on the job.

You need to understand your purpose and you need to understand the time when you are going to fulfil it. Not only that, you must also know what exactly to do when the season is fully ripe.

Let's go back to the script again. When you read it, what is in the heart of the producer will be made known to you. The word of God says the Lord God is a sun and shield; no good thing will He withhold from those who walk uprightly before Him. His word also says that the earth and the fullness thereof are His. If you are working for God and faithfully serving Him, He will reward you. You can only know that when you take time to read the script. It is what will let you know the heart of the producer and what your future on the job would look like.

God showed Joseph his future before he got there and he did not take any free gift that didn't come from God. Should Joseph had accepted the offer of Potiphar's wife, he would have forfeited his destiny. Gehazi lost both ways; he never fulfilled his purpose and never enjoyed what he requested for in greed.

> '...*Is this the time to take money or to accept clothes...? Naaman's leprosy will cling to you and to your descendants forever." Then Gehazi went from Elisha's presence and his skin was leprous—it had become as white as snow.'* 2 Kings 5:26-27(NIV)

The children of Issachar were a direct opposite of Gehazi. They had a very good picture of times and seasons and they knew what they should do. That is the

If you are working for God and faithfully serving Him, He will reward you.

perfect combination. They were part of the people that came to David to make him king. What a beautiful gift for his life! That is why the prayer of Moses is still so relevant. May God bring you to your own people, and may they not be few! Of all the men that came to make David king, the Bible highlighted their distinctive features; their understanding of the times and the purpose attached to those seasons.

When you have such men on your team or come across them in your path you are truly blessed. They will not focus on what is irrelevant to your role and once it is the appropriate time to set the camera rolling they will cheer you on to play your part on the stage at that very particular time.

> *'...from Issachar, men who understood the times and knew what Israel should do...'*-1 Chronicles 12:32(NIV)

Jonah wanted to do the work of God on his own terms. He was reluctant to go to where God wanted him to go. He predicted that the aim of his mission would be unprofitable. He did not fully comprehend that his purpose was time bound. God wanted him in Nineveh at that point in time to avoid wiping out the entire nation. What would have happened if Jonah did not go to Nineveh? He wanted to excuse himself from his assignment and as a result put other people's lives in jeopardy. He opted for a place that God wouldn't have to stay at that point in time. Don't forget that the location for your role is as important as the role itself. That explains why locations are meticulously selected in the production of a movie. In fact a professional is assigned to secure the appropriate locations where a particular production will take place.

More often than not, the location contains the necessary set and props needed for the interpretation of a role. At the point of sending Jonah to Nineveh, God wanted that nation to return to Him in ashes and sackcloth. He wanted them to be saved from peril.

Today, as an intercessor, you can have a nudging in your heart to pray for a nation being plunged into sin because of its political system. God is constantly calling men to repentance and He uses different methods in reaching out to lost souls. He can urge you to preach to a colleague at work, arrange picnics for the youths in a neighbourhood just to reach out to them and save them.

Your assignment can become irrelevant if you don't embrace it at the right season. Of what use is praying for an event after it has taken place and destroyed lives and left nations in turmoil?

> Your assignment can become irrelevant if you don't embrace it at the right season.

Timing is very important in fulfilling purpose. This weighty truth cannot be overemphasized. Failure to pray at a specific time that God put in your heart might spell doom for the people involved. Great disasters have been avoided just because somebody somewhere was there at his duty post where the clarion call came. If not for God's intervention, Jonah would have lost the opportunity of fulfilling purpose. God gave him a

133

second chance. I will address that subject extensively in the next chapter.

The Master showed us a very perfect example of purpose and timing. At the marriage ceremony in Cana of Galilee, His mother wanted Him to do whatever He could do to supply more wine for the wedding-but this request wasn't at the appropriate time and He declined. He had a perfect understanding of what needed to be done and when it should be done.

> **"Woman, why do you involve me?" Jesus replied. "My hour has not yet come."** John 2:4(NIV)

I want to use a very practical example here. As a parent, you have a purpose; a role to play in the lives of your children. This role will change as the season in their lives change. It would look something like this:

Children's age Your role

Age 0-15 - A guardian
Age 15-30 - A friend
Age 30 and above - A mentor

The role you are meant to play must be clearly stated and you must strictly adhere to what is expected of you per season, otherwise it will be very difficult to catch up in latter years.

The danger of procrastination

Sometimes we all know we have amazing things to do for God but more often than not we shy away from it. We run because it is daunting or we wait endlessly for the perfect time to get it done. Have you been putting off what needs to be done now for a more 'convenient time?' That is called procrastination. If you want to make the most of your days you must avoid it like a

 It is only what you get accomplished in God's time that is truly beautiful!

plague.

How to overcome procrastination

1. Ask God for the grace to fulfil your purpose and overcome it
2. Cultivate discipline
3. Always do the most difficult tasks first. If you put in the big stones into a jar, the small ones will easily fit in. if you do it the other way round, it is going to be difficult. Once the major assignment has been carried out, the less important ones will be very cheap to achieve

4. Break large roles into smaller chunks. You will notice that a film is broken into acts and scenes. A large mountain is a combination of a lot of elements. Your body is one but it has many parts functioning together to form a whole.

It is only what you get accomplished in God's time that is truly beautiful!

'To everything there is a season, and a time to every purpose under the heaven: a time to be born, and a time to die; a time to plant, and a time to pluck up that which is planted. A time to kill, and a time to heal; a time to break down, and a time to build up; a time to weep, and a time to laugh; a time to mourn, and a time to dance. A time to cast away stones, and a time to gather stones together; a time to embrace, and a time to refrain from embracing; a time to get, and a time to lose; a time to keep, and a time to cast away. A time to rend, and a time to sew; a time to keep silence, and a time to speak. A time to love, and a time to hate, a time of war, and a time of peace. He hath made everything beautiful in his time...' Ecclesiastes 3:1-8, 11.

OVERVIEW

You don't have the whole of eternity to make a mark. You won't be here forever. Time counts in fulfilling purpose and not a single second must be wasted. There is a season; a time when your assignment must get done.

REFLECTION

I)   Do you have a daily 'to do' list?
ii)   Do you have targets? Do you take time to draft long and short term goals? If you don't, you will be like a footballer playing on a football field without a goal post. Don't forget 'nothing ventured; nothing gained.'

INDELIBLE MARKS

"Nothing in the world is worth having or worth doing unless it means effort, pain, difficulty... I have never in my life envied a human being who led an easy life. I have envied a great many people who led difficult lives and led them well."
— *Theodore Roosevelt*

INDELIBLE MARKS

They came, they saw, they conquered
I saw their footprints but their faces I never knew
I saw their blood on my Bible
They gave their lives to get it published
I saw their sweat on the pages
They spent countless years to get it translated
Now I can have many translations in just one language
I was told there was a time
The saints locked the door to only read just a page;
endlessly for days
Now I can read as often as I want
Thank God they came
They constructed bridges
I can go anywhere I want
Riding on what they accomplished
They wrote books
They built hospitals
They wiped tears and made the world better
They invented great machines
They discovered the cure for ailments

Thank God for these great souls
Who walked before me
May others coming behind
Be able to thank God that I came!

There's nothing you do for the Lord that will not count for life and eternity. When you fulfil the purpose God has carved out for you, it will leave a mark; an impact that cannot be forgotten in a hurry. The sweet epitaph seen on most graves are nothing in comparison to what purpose really is. It is not what men say about you that matters as what God says concerning you. The lives you

  The beauty of life is not in how long but how well. Enjoying a long duration is good but enjoying a purpose-filled life is even better.

affected, and the change that was birthed because you fulfilled your purpose are the real deal. Most of the time, they are things that people cannot fully grasp. The beauty of life is not in how long but how well. Enjoying a long duration is good but enjoying a purpose-filled life is even better.

'When Enoch had lived 65 years, he became the father of Methuselah. After he became the father of Methuselah, Enoch walked faithfully with God 300 years and had other sons and daughters. Altogether, Enoch lived a total of

141

365 years. Enoch walked faithfully with God; then he was no more, because God took him away. When Methuselah had lived 187 years, he became the father of Lamech. After he became the father of Lamech, Methuselah lived 782 years and had other sons and daughters. Altogether, Methuselah lived a total of 969 years, and then he died.' Genesis 5:21-27(NIV)

When Jesus came, He spent the first thirty years of His life in preparation for what He came to do.

In all the record of his life, Methuselah did not do anything apart from giving birth. In all his nine hundred and sixty nine years, all he did was father children. Nothing else was said about his destiny, his purpose and the changes he effected. The only thing recorded against his name is being the man that lived the longest on the face of the earth.

When Jesus came, He spent the first thirty years of His life in preparation for what He came to do. The next three and a half years were spent in executing His God ordained purpose. His name and deeds are on the lips of every tongue, two thousand years after and still counting. He brought salvation to mankind through the shedding of His blood. The result has been bringing countless souls to God on a daily basis; now that is a life well spent. The duration of His life and assignment are in sharp contrast to Methuselah's. Life is not about duration but largely about donation.

Many saints of old lived long and fulfilled purpose. Moses, Joshua and Abraham lived long and lived well. The duration of a man's life is ultimately God's decision while the man determines how the days given to him are spent. The choice is ultimately ours to make the most of our days and make something meaningful of our lives. Life is really not about duration but about donation.

This is what the Bible says about some saints of old; it is a chronicle of how they ended their journey here on earth:

David

> *'David son of Jesse was king over all Israel. He ruled over Israel forty years—seven in Hebron and thirty-three in Jerusalem. He died at a good old age, having enjoyed long life, wealth and honour. His son Solomon succeeded him as king'* 1 Chronicles 29:26-28(NIV)

Abraham

'Abraham was now very old, and the Lord had blessed him in every way.' Genesis 24:1 (NIV)

'Then Abraham breathed his last and died at a good old age, an old man and full of years; and he was gathered to his people. His sons Isaac and Ishmael buried him in the cave of Machpelah near Mamre, in the field of Ephron son of Zohar the Hittite." Genesis 25:8-9 (NIV)

Moses

'Moses was a hundred and twenty years old when he died, yet his eyes were not weak nor his strength gone.' Deuteronomy 34:7 (NIV)

Isaac

'Isaac lived a hundred and eighty years. [29] Then he breathed his last and died and was gathered to his people, old and full of years. And his sons Esau and Jacob buried him.' Genesis 35:28-29 (NIV)

Jacob

'When Jacob had finished giving instructions to his sons, he drew his feet up into the bed, breathed his last and was gathered to his people.' Genesis 49:33 (NIV)

Joshua

*'When Joshua had grown old, the Lord said to him, "You are now very old, and there are still very large areas of land to be taken over.'*Joshua 13:1(NIV)

*'"Now then, just as the Lord promised, He has kept me alive for forty-five years since the time He said this to Moses, while Israel moved about in the wilderness. So here I am today, eighty-five years old! I am still as strong today as the day Moses sent me out; I'm just as vigorous to go out to battle now as I was then. Now give me this hill country that the Lord promised me that day. You yourself heard then that the Anakites were there and their cities were large and fortified, but, the Lord helping me, I will drive them out just as He said."'*Joshua 14:10-12(NIV)

*'Joshua son of Nun, the servant of the Lord, died at the age of a hundred and ten. And they buried him in the land of his inheritance, at Timnathheres in the hill country of Ephraim, north of Mount Gaash..'*Judges 2:8-9(NIV)

Caleb

Then Joshua blessed Caleb son of Jephunneh and gave him Hebron as his inheritance. So Hebron has belonged to Caleb son of

145

Jephunneh the Kenizzite ever since, because he followed the Lord, the God of Israel, wholeheartedly. 'Joshua 14:13-14(NIV)

This is the end of the righteous:

'Mark the perfect man, and behold the upright for the end of that man is peace.' Psalms 37:37. (KJV)

'Say ye to the righteous, that it shall be well with him: for they shall eat the fruit of their doings.' Isaiah 3:10. (KJV)

'The righteous shall flourish like the palm tree: he shall grow like a cedar in Lebanon. Those that be planted in the house of the Lord shall flourish in the courts of our God. They shall still bring forth fruit in old age; they shall be fat and flourishing.' Psalms 92:12-14. (KJV)

Life is not about duration but largely about donation.

Carefully reading these scriptures will open your eyes to discover amazing things. The men of old did outstanding things. Some of them were conquering new territories in their old age. Most of them handed over the baton to the generation after them and blessed

Locating your script in the scripture

their children. They released the blessings of God upon their lives to be able to carry on the work and prosper like they did. Because they fulfilled purpose they enjoyed the wealth that came via the covenant of Abraham.

We can enjoy the same grace. We can fight and conquer. We are able to leave our footprints on the sands of time. There could be something about our names that will point the next generation to greater heights. We can do exploits for God! No city is too strong to take. No nation is too mighty to subdue. We know that through God we have the ability to do valiantly.

You may be asking 'what if I strayed in my walk?' God is the God of a second chance. You can rise again after a fall.

> *...for though the righteous fall seven times, they rise again, but the wicked stumble when calamity strikes"*- Proverbs 24:16

God is a God of mercy. When He forgives He throws the sins into the sea of forgetfulness. Jonah was hidden in the belly of the fish and God sorted him out to fulfil his destiny. No matter how far gone you think you are, God can restore you.

In spite of wreaking havoc in the past against the

147

church, Paul became a mighty instrument that is still speaking to the church today although he is long dead. Your life counts and can still turn men to God. You can overcome that addiction and start a foundation that will address the same challenge.

No matter how filthy your sins are, the blood of Jesus will wash you and make you as white as snow. Just like the prodigal son, you can come back home because the Father has longed for you since the very first day you left. You have always been in His heart. He will be glad to have you back in fellowship with Him. What matters is

No matter how far gone you think you are, God can restore you.

not the number of times you fell but how quickly you rose up again to continue the journey. Nothing matters at all; the only thing that matters is being able to cross the finish line and getting the trophy.

In the course of carrying out his assignment, Paul encountered imprisonment, shipwreck and betrayal from Christian brethren. Through the entire ordeal he did not shift his eyes from the goal. He did not lose focus on his mission. In fact he looked forward to being afflicted; he was prepared for what might come his way and in advance he told himself he would not allow anything whatsoever to prevent him from fulfilling his God ordained destiny. He was ready to die for the work that was committed to his hands. How prepared are you to weather the storms you might encounter in the course of fulfilling destiny?

> *'I only know that in every city the Holy Spirit warns me that prison and hardships are facing me. However, I consider my life worth nothing to me; my only aim is to finish the race and complete the task the Lord Jesus has given me—the task of testifying to the good news of God's grace.'* Acts 20:23-24 (NIV)

What are you living for? After your death what will you be remembered for? Great names like the Wright brothers, Thomas Edison, Helen Keller and Mother Theresa, to mention just a few, are known for something tangible. They found their scripts and they played their individual roles as given to them.

Have you located your script? Do you know the role you've been given to play? Let your voice be heard. Play your role well that it affects the lives of others positively. Play it so well that at the end of it all, when the curtain falls or the Director says, "That's a wrap", you will bow with pride as you receive a standing ovation.

Like Paul the apostle, at the end of your sojourn here, may you be able to say 'I have fought a good fight, I have

149

finished my course, I have kept the faith!'

THERE ARE THINGS TO DO AND PLACES TO GO; GOD'S SPIRIT BECKONS!

OVERVIEW

You must leave a mark on the sands of time. Something must get done as a result of being born on earth. Your name must leave a mark of something being added to make life meaningful for those coming after you.

REFLECTION

I)   If you die today, apart from the sweet words on the condolence register and carefully engraved words on your grave what will people sincerely miss about you? Would they wish they could turn back the hands of time and have you live just one more day?

ing Source UK Ltd.
UK
1215
K00001B/165/P